"Giora Eliraz's book represents a valuable addition to the all too sparse collection of scholarly writing on Islam in the world's largest Muslim nation. With very few exceptions, most such studies are the work of area specialists with a deep understanding of their country of study but comparatively little knowledge of the Middle East. Eliraz's book is very different; it is the fruit of a sharp academic mind honed through decades of study of the intellectual history of the Arab world. The result is a very well informed study uniquely enriched by the ability to read developments in Southeast Asia from a Middle Eastern perspective. Consequently anyone seeking to understand Indonesian Islam and its global context will benefit from this work – regardless of whether they are seasoned observers or are coming to this increasingly important subject for the first time."

Greg Barton,
Deakin University, Australia

"With the growth of armed Islamic movements in the Middle East, and with the overthrow of the authoritarian Soeharto regime in May 1998, observers of global Muslim affairs have been curious to see whether Indonesia, the world's largest Muslim-majority country, might be about to experience its own process of religious radicalization. The growth of armed paramilitaries after Soeharto's overthrow and the Bali bombings in October 2002 seemed to confirm that Muslim politics in this once tolerant country was indeed being radicalized. In this well-written book, however, Giora Eliraz provides a more thoughtful and, ultimately, hopeful prognosis. Already an accomplished scholar of Middle Eastern Islam before turning to Indonesian affairs, Eliraz demonstrates that a radical fringe has long existed in Indonesia, and occasionally made serious mischief. However, with a careful and comparative eye, Eliraz shows that the mainstream of the Muslim community remains unswervingly moderate. Equally intriguing, Eliraz's knowledge of

Islamic reform in Egypt and elsewhere in the Middle East allows him to bring original and often startling insights to his Indonesian materials, as when he demonstrates that the ideas of the great Egyptian reformer Muhammad Abduh took deeper root in the Indonesian landscape than they did in Abduh's homeland. His comparative analyses of the growth of Islamic radicalism in contemporary Indonesia – and the vigorous response it provoked among Muslim moderates – are equally stimulating and original. Carefully researched and engagingly written, this fine book deserves to be read by everyone interested in Indonesian Islam, as well as by the general reader curious about the varieties and future of Muslim politics."

Robert W. Hefner,
Professor of Anthropology,
Associate Director of the Institute on Culture, Religion
and World Affairs (CURA), Boston University

"Islam in Indonesia has long been regarded by many observers and scholars of Islam as an impure and syncretic Islam. In the last two decades, however, this misconception has been corrected through a number of important studies which take a comparative approach when looking at how different Muslim societies function in today's world. Giora Eliraz's *Islam in Indonesia* is an excellent contribution to understanding the complex connection and links between Indonesian Islam with that of the Middle East. This study is very timely indeed when the international public is eager to obtain credible knowledge on the origins and root causes of radicalism among limited groups of Muslims in Indonesia in recent years."

Azyumardi Azra,
Professor of History and Rector
of State Islamic University Jakarta, Indonesia,
and Professorial Fellow at University of Melbourne, Australia

Islam in Indonesia

To my wife
Bati

Islam in Indonesia

MODERNISM, RADICALISM, AND THE MIDDLE EAST DIMENSION

Giora Eliraz

sussex
ACADEMIC
PRESS

BRIGHTON • PORTLAND

2 4 6 8 10 9 7 5 3 1

First published 2004 in Great Britain by
SUSSEX ACADEMIC PRESS
PO Box 2950
Brighton BN2 5SP

and in the United States of America by
SUSSEX ACADEMIC PRESS
920 NE 58th Ave   Suite 300
Portland, Oregon 97213–3786

British Library Cataloguing in Publication Data
A CIP catalogue record for this book is available from the British Library.

Library of Congress Cataloging-in-Publication Data
Eliraz, Giora.
    Islam in Indonesia : modernism, radicalism, and
the Middle East dimension / Giora Eliraz.
        p. cm.
    Includes bibliographical references and index.
    ISBN 1-84519-040-8 (hardcover : alk. paper)
    1. Islam—Indonesia—21st century. 2. Islamic
renewal—Indonesia. 3. Islam and politics—
Indonesia. 4. Indonesia—Politics and government.
5. Religion and politics—Indonesia. 6. Indonesia—
Relations—Middle East. 7. Middle East—
Relations—Indonesia. I. Title.
BP63.I5E45 2004
297′.09598′090511—dc22
                                                    2004013010
                                                    CIP

Typeset and designed by G&G Editorial, Brighton
Printed by The Cromwell Press, Trowbridge, Wiltshire
This book is printed on acid-free paper.

Contents

Contents

Preface

The topic of Islam in Southeast Asia has long been marginalized in the fields of Islamic studies and Southeast Asian studies. As Robert W. Hefner writes, "Western and Middle Eastern scholars alike have tended to place Southeast Asia at the intellectual periphery of the Islamic world."[1] Indonesia is the home of the largest Muslim community in the world and in the aftermath of the of growing attention, worldwide, that has been given post-September 11 to manifestations of radical Islam in the Islamic world, and following the Bali bombings of October 12, 2002, Islam in Indonesia has ostensibly gained more attention in the media. Naturally, much of this attention has been strictly limited to current affairs. The noticeable disregard of Islam in Indonesia in the Western media has cleared the way for a selective observation of its influence and development.

This book addresses two contemporary case studies in the field of Islam in Indonesia. The first is that of the Islamic modernist movement in the Malay-Indonesian world in the first decades of the twentieth century. The second case study is that of current radical Islamic fundamentalism in Indonesia. Both strands are examined in light of the wider Islamic perspective and the contemporary history of the Middle East. Even though Indonesia is a remote periphery of the Islamic world, Islam in the Indonesian archipelago is strongly connected to the hub of Islamic civilization. Similarly, it has shown itself for years to be highly attentive to the varying ideas and streams of thoughts in the "center" of the Islamic world. Hence, the impact that the Middle East has had on Islam in Indonesia is significant. This impact has continued to grow in the modern era.

Even though the Middle Eastern perspective is widely employed throughout the book, it is not done so from a conventional scholarly position which portrays Islam in Indonesia, and indeed in the entire Malay Indonesian world, as a mere derivative of the Middle East. Certain Islamic ideas and streams of thoughts diffused to Indonesia from the "center" of the Islamic world, once on Indonesian soil, underwent some modifications. The local context in Indonesia marks itself on the "Islamic space" there, exhibiting its own unique character. Therefore, attention is also given to the particularities of the local Indonesian context and the uniqueness of its own "Islamic space".

The book suggests the local–Middle Eastern Islamic praxis as an enriching methodological tool for the field of research on Islam in Indonesia. **Chapter I** examines the narrative of Islamic modernism in the Malay-Indonesian world, which is tightly connected with the Middle East, and in particular with Egypt. In Egypt, toward the end of the nineteenth century, Muhammad 'Abduh (1849–1905) laid the conceptual foundations of Islamic modernism, following the spirit of his mentor and colleague, Jamal al-Din al-Afghani (1839–97). In the first decades of the twentieth century the ideas of this Islamic modernism found their way, through various mechanisms of dissemination, to the Malay-Indonesian world, where they fired the imagination of Indonesian youth and developed over time into a massive, challenging and influential movement. By examining the formative phase of Islamic modernism in the Malay-Indonesian world, through its Middle Eastern roots, an informative comparative viewpoint can be articulated.

The second and the third chapters of the book are focused on the subject of radical Islamic fundamentalism in Indonesia. **Chapter 2** examines the globalized dimension of radical Islam. Radical Islamic fundamentalism in Indonesia is a local case of a multi-dimensional global phenomenon. The methodological approach in this chapter utilizes two kinds of perspectives, serving as two complementary lenses. The first is the current perspective, which is directed toward the ideology of the radical Islamic fundamentalist groups in Indonesia and the transmission of radical Islamic ideas from the Middle East to Indonesia. The second is a broader historical perspective, directed mainly toward the Islamic conceptual interaction between Indonesia and the Middle East, including the role played by various cultural brokers, and which has been carried out through a multifocal cross-regional and global process of the transferring of ideas. The study of this interaction, which has taken place through the centuries between the two regions, reveals much about the current phenomenon of radical Islamic fundamentalism in Indonesia.

Chapter 3 analyzes radical Islamic fundamentalism in Indonesia. The guiding postulate in this discussion is that unlike the prominence of radical Islamic fundamentalism in many Muslim countries, in the Middle East in particular, radical fundamentalism in Indonesia is marginal one, since it represents there a tiny minority only and its creed has failed to attract the majority of Indonesian Muslims. This fact is even more amazing when one considers Indonesian polity and society through the eyes of a hypothetical fundamentalist from the Middle East. The reasons for the apparently amazing marginality of radical Islamic fundamentalism in Indonesia are established through structuring a panoramic view of Islam in Indonesia. Through this panoramic view, the particularities and the distinctive traits and texture of the Islamic context are revealed.

The contemporary distinguished Indonesian intellectual, Azyumardi Azra, argues that there is a tendency among scholars to exclude the Malay-Indonesian world from any discussion of Islam, since it is situated on the periphery of the Muslim world. Islam in the archipelago has long been regarded as not being "real Islam" and it is considered distant from Islam in the centers in the Middle East. Azra adds that even though the local influence on Islam in the archipelago cannot be ignored, "one should not assume that the Malay-Indonesian Islamic tradition has little to do with Islam in the Middle East".[2] In this sense this study calls for the relevancy of research on Islam in Indonesia in terms of Islam in the "center" of the world of Islam. This relevancy is not only established on the similarities which are revealed through a comparative view. The particularities of the "Islamic space" in the Indonesian archipelago will provide challenging insights for research on Islamic societies and culture.

GIORA ELIRAZ

FACULTY OF ASIAN STUDIES, THE AUSTRALIAN NATIONAL UNIVERSITY
CANBERRA, 2003

THE HEBREW UNIVERSITY OF JERUSALEM, 2004

Acknowledgments

This book is the result of research which was conducted at the Australian National University. I would like to express my gratitude to Dr George Quinn, Professor Virginia Hooker, and Professor Anthony Milner for giving me the precious opportunity to stay at the ANU as a Visiting Fellow and for greatly encouraging me in my work.

I owe much to Professor Robert Hefner for giving me encouragement in my efforts to cut my own path in the field of Islam in Indonesia. I also wish to express my thanks to Professor Aharon Layish and Professor Amnon Cohen who supported my idea of entering this fascinating field of knowledge and research.

I am most grateful to Dr Wendy Mukherjee and Dr Christine Campbell for being a tremendous help in refining the manuscript. For that, and also for their significant comments and their unique friendly support, I wish to offer special thanks.

I wish to thank Professor Emmanuel Sivan for offering his enlightening comments on early drafts of the manuscript, and for his inspiration. I also wish to express my appreciation to Dr Greg Barton and Badrus Sholeh for providing valuable comments. Professor Raphael Israeli has been supportive, and I thank him for his role in promoting the publication of this book. I would like to express my thanks to The Harry S. Truman Research Institute for the Advancement of Peace at The Hebrew University of Jerusalem for providing financial support in the publication of this work.

I am grateful to *Studia Islamika* (Indonesian Journal for Islamic Studies) for permission to include in this book a revised version of an article of mine, previously published in vol. 9, no. 2 of *Studia Islamika*.

Last but not least, I am extremely indebted and enormously grateful to my wife Bati. Obliged to stay far away from Australia, due to her demanding family responsibilities, she was a wonderfully supportive, encouraging and attentive partner all along the way.

1

The Islamic Modernist Movement in the Malay-Indonesian World

A Comparative Look at Egypt

It needed only one *haji* to return from the Middle East fired with reformist ideas, one religious teacher to study at a *Kaum Muda* madrassah in Singapore, Perak or Penang, to divide a village temporarily into two embittered factions.

(William R. Roff)

The narrative of the Islamic modernist movement, also known as the Islamic reformist movement, in the Malay-Indonesian world is a significant voice in the modern history of Islam in the region. The first four decades of the twentieth century were particularly fruitful, mainly because this period of time was closely interwoven with the fierce conflict between the *Kaum Muda* ("young group"), the modernists/reformists, and the *Kaum Tua* ("old group"), the traditionalists.

Examined from a broad perspective, this chapter in the modern history of Islam in the Malay-Indonesian world constitutes a remarkable milestone in the continuous and substantial influence of the Islamic Middle East on Southeast Asia. In von der Mehden's view, the modernist movement was the intellectual import from the Middle East with the greatest impact on public Islam in Southeast Asia during the century before World War II.[1] Deliar Noer has asserted, referring to the first four decades of the twentieth century, that reformist ideas like those of Muhammad 'Abduh and Rashid Rida fired the imagination of Indonesian youth.[2] The narrative of the Islamic modernist movement in the Malay-Indonesian world is, without question, intimately and deeply connected with the Middle East in general, and with Egypt in particular.

The transmission of Islamic modernist ideas from the Middle East to the Malay-Indonesian world can be traced by taking a comparative look at Egypt, one of Islam's central strongholds. Hence, through a comparative view that links the "center" of the Islamic world with its alleged "periphery", an attempt will be made to generate insights about this transmission and development of the Islamic modernist movement in the Malay-Indonesian world.

Muhammad 'Abduh's Heritage

Towards the end of the nineteenth century, Muhammad 'Abduh (1849–1905) systematically laid the conceptual foundations of the Islamic modernist movement in Egypt, following in the spirit of his mentor and colleague, Jamal al-Din al-Afghani (1839–97). But the conceptual heritage he left behind has been subject to contradictory interpretations. This is mainly due to its being, in part, an ambiguous formula, which suggests harmony in true Islam between the religious claim "to express God's will about how men should live in society" and the "irreversible movement of modern civilization",[3] or between revelation and the Tradition of the Prophet, on the one hand, and human reason and science on the other hand.[4] After the death of 'Abduh the delicate conceptual balance he created was overturned by his followers. One group was inspired by the Syrian Rashid Rida (1865–1935), who made Egypt his home from 1897 and became 'Abduh's prominent disciple, biographer, and the spokesman of his ideas. Rida was also the founder and editor of the successful Cairo-based journal *al-Manar* (1898–1935). He used it as an organ for promulgating 'Abduh's reformist ideas, taking his heritage in the direction of a puritan approach, and calling for a return to the strict values and ideals of the *salaf* (from *al-salaf al-salih*, the "righteous forefathers"), and to the purist origins of the *Qur'an* and the *Sunna*. H. A. R. Gibb says that in the pages of *al-Manar*, the followers of this group even replaced the influence of the "great conciliator", al-Ghazali, with that of the "fundamentalist",

Ibn Taimiya.[5] Known as the *salafiyya* movement, they imbued 'Abduh's insistence on the unchanging nature and absolute claims of essential Islam with an orientation of Hanbali fundamentalism. Other followers of 'Abduh developed his emphasis on the legitimacy of social change into a de facto division between two realms: religion and society.[6] Nadav Safran states that 'Abduh's ideology and program, as a whole, gained support in Egypt only among a tiny group of reformers; however, some of his ideas have had a considerable influence on Egyptian Islamic thought and development. Much of that thought and literature, Safran adds, carried some of 'Abduh's ideas far beyond what he had intended, while "both schools could lay claim to his authority because his thought did indeed lend itself easily to radical and conservative interpretations".[7] Malcolm H. Kerr points out that the great moral purpose of practical reform that characterized Islamic modernism at the turn of the twentieth century was quietly dissipated. Modernism's adherents have found other homes, explains Kerr, at either end of the nationalism–conservatism spectrum, and thus the dissipation has scarcely been noticed. No one in Egypt "is heard today mourning the legacy of Muhammad 'Abduh: on the contrary, everyone claims it as his own. The difficulty is that the teachings of 'Abduh and his circle rested on intellectual foundations that were, on the whole, vague and unsystematic."[8]

This tradition of Islamic modernism – inspired initially by Jamal al-Din al-Afghani, formulated in essence mainly by Muhammad 'Abduh, and carried on and interpreted by Rashid Rida – constituted the dominant breeding ground of the Islamic modernist movement in the Malay-Indonesian world. It is there that the Islamic modernist heritage, transmitted to a large extent from Egypt, one of the main active historical centers of Islamic modernist thought in the Islamic world, was planted, and grew in the early twentieth century into an influential movement. This movement retained, then, the authentic features of the original Islamic modernist heritage, including its motivations, fundamentals, and terminology. During the first decades of the twentieth century the Malay-Indonesian Islamic modernist movement began to introduce innovations into this heritage.

The Challenge of the Islamic Modernist Movement in the Malay-Indonesian World

When observing the early Islamic modernist movement in the Malay-Indonesian world, one is struck by the strength of the religious, social, and political challenges it posed, which threatened, primarily, the various "guardians" of the region's traditional values and institutions. This challenge, which generated the *Kaum Muda–Kaum Tua* conflict between the Islamic modernists and the traditionalists, was salient mainly in Indonesia, then the Dutch East Indies, and the three British colonies known as the Straits Settlements (consisting of Singapore, Penang, and Malacca). In British Malaya, despite its geographic proximity to the Straits Settlements, Islamic modernism failed to take a strong hold.[9]

The Reformist Motivation

Jamal al-Din al-Afghani and Muhammad 'Abduh's diagnosis of the "inner decay" of Islamic societies and their "backwardness",[10] which motivated their reformist drive, clearly had an impact on the initial motivating power of the modernists in the Malay-Indonesian world. The Islamic modernist journal, *al-Imam* (1906–8), was the first newspaper that carried the message of Islamic modernism in the Malay-Muslim world. It was based in Singapore, which together with Penang formed "the intellectual nerve-centers of the Islamic renaissance" in Southeast Asia.[11] The journal was greatly influenced by the Islamic modernist ideas of the Egyptian *al-Manar* and was closely modeled on it.[12] *Al-Imam* analyzed the ills of Malay society in a manner and language resembling al-Afghani and Muhammad 'Abduh's diagnosis of the state of Islamic society, pointing to "the 'backwardness' of the Malays, their domination by aliens, their ignorance of modern fields of knowledge, their laziness, their complacency, their feuds among themselves and inability to cooperate".[13] These failings of the Malay, argued *al-Imam*, were shared by the whole Islamic world, a natural consequence of ignoring the commands of God.[14] Similarly, Kijahi Hadji Ahmad Dahlan, the founder of Muhammadiyah – the Islamic modernist organization founded in Jogjakarta in 1912 and still a major force in the narrative of the Islamic modernist movement in the Malay-Indonesian world – was motivated by the realization that Indonesian Muslims were in a state of decline and undergoing a crisis of faith.[15] Since Dahlan was inspired by Jamal al-Din al-Afghani and Muhammad 'Abduh's thought, it is not surprising at all to find the conceptual imprint of both of these men in his reformist drive.

The Religious Dimension

In essence, the message of the Islamic modernist movement is grounded in the religious sphere, in a search for salvation and for answers within Islam to the crisis of Islamic society. The remedy to the crisis can be found by revealing the truths of Islam, purifying its commandments, and obeying them. Consequently, the Islamic modernist movement in the Malay-Indonesian world followed the steps of its predecessors' ideas in the Middle East, initially placed mainly in the religious sphere. Notwithstanding, some other important dimensions – educational, social, and political – also became evident in the actions and thought of the Islamic modernist movement in the Malay-Indonesian world. Since it bore a reformist religious message and a puritan orientation, Islamic modernism ran counter to the world-view of the greater part of the diversified Muslim communities in the Malay-Indonesian world, which were located at different points on the imaginary line extending from the orthodox Islamic pole, on the one hand, and syncretic Islam on the other hand. Primarily, two provocative fundamental tenets stand at the center of the religious platform of Islamic modernism.

The first tenet is the theological call for *ijtihad*, the individual and independent rational-legal interpretation of theological questions based on the *Qur'an* and the *hadith*. It was proposed as a legal mechanism in lieu of the *taklid*, blind and uncritical acceptance of the theological interpretations of the great masters of the past, namely those of the four schools of canon law: *al-madhahib*. A strict adherence of the traditionalists to the methods of interpretation and the teachings of the four classical schools of Islamic jurisprudence was even presented in Indonesia by the modernist Muslims as the prime cause for the stagnation of Muslim religious life and consequently the cause for their loss of political power. The *ijtihad* was vigorously championed by the Islamic modernists in the Malay-Indonesian world. This concept carried a call, in accordance with 'Abduh's concept, to utilize *'aql* (reasoning) in reference to worldly matters in order to apply the prescriptions laid down in the *Qur'an* and the *hadith* to contemporary conditions and demands, in contrast to the unchanging nature of the essentials of the divine doctrine and prophecy. The modernist Muslims held the opinion that the *ijtihad* had to carried out by the religious scholars and specialists, not by laymen. In the spirit of *ijtihad*, the Muhammadiyah established, in 1927, a council of prominent religious scholars, called *Madjlis Tardjih*, in order to consider matters of religious belief and practice.[16]

The second tenet of Islamic modernism is a decisive demand to purify Islamic doctrine and practice from *bid'a*, heretical and improper "innovation", namely those accretions of practices and beliefs that historically lack Islamic justification, such as non-Islamic mysticism, magic and superstition, as well as animist, Hindu, and Buddhist elements that had been incorporated into Islam in Southeast Asia.[17] In the spirit of this tenet modernist Muslims in Malay-Indonesia attacked, among other things, the use of magic and charms by the Sufi orders, the *tarekat*. This demand for total purification of Islamic doctrine and practice was one of the main reasons for the conflict between the *Kaum Muda,* and the *Kaum Tua.* The conflict included various issues, among them the basic dichotomy between the "*shari'a*-mindedness" of the modernists, to use Marshall G. S. Hodgson's phrase,[18] who claimed to be governed by Islamic law in all aspects of life, and the *adat*, or local traditions and customs. The *adat*, which were accepted by sizeable segments of Indonesian Muslims, prominent among them the Javanese *abangan* (the syncretist nominal Muslims, as opposed to the *santri*, the orthodox Muslims), were regarded by the modernists as remnants of animist or Hindu-Buddhist traditions. One of the issues that aroused heated disputes was also the modernist Muslims' rejection of the *usalli* (Arabic: *niya*), the pronouncement of the formulation of intention at the beginning of the prayer. Another controversial issue, also rejected by the modernists on the grounds of its being *bid'a*, was the reciting of the *talqin* ("instruction"), the short address spoken over the grave at burial, consisting of advice to the dead about how to reply during their questioning by the angels. The acceptance by Muhammadiyah of the principle that the Friday sermon could be conducted in the vernacular, rather than in Arabic, was in opposition to the traditional orthodox position.[19] Muhammadiyah has also been striving for years to purify the lives of its members of the major traditional Javanese rituals. This applies to the major ritual complexes around which "the existence of the Javanese has been organized for a millennium":[20] *slametan* (the ritual feast shared by neighbors), which is at the core of the entire Javanese religious system; *wayang* (the shadow play with leather puppets); and *hormat*, the various rituals for venerating rank. In rejecting the *hormat,* which expresses the deeply rooted Javanese tradition of emphasizing hierarchy and status, the modernist Muslims were largely motivated by a basic premise in Islam, and in Islamic modernism in particular, that all believers are equal in the eyes of God.[21] At the same time, Muhammadiyah, which declares itself as a movement for *dakwah islamiya amar ma'ruf nahi munkar* ("Islamic missionary activity calling for commanding right and forbidden wrong"),[22] tried to promote among Muslims those practices and beliefs it regards as religiously correct.

The Educational Dimension

The Islamic modernist efforts in the field of education also posed a threat to traditionalists in the Malay-Indonesian world. These efforts were largely motivated by a basic interest, inspired by Muhammad 'Abduh's ideas, in improving the level of religious education, and in modernizing the educational system in order to adapt it to pressing contemporary needs. Hence, a type of modern school, *madrasa*, was established by the Islamic modernist movement, both by organizations and individuals, in the Indonesian archipelago and in the Malay peninsula. This type of school was a reaction to the old-fashioned Islamic school, *pondok* or *pesantren*. The traditional method of teaching, the *halaqa* ("study group"), where students, irrespective of age, sat in a circle around the teacher and learnt the material by rote, was dropped; a new classroom method was introduced by the modernists. Now the students sat in rows, used graded texts, and were encouraged to participate actively in the class. In addition to the religious subjects, secular subjects were also included in the curriculum. In Indonesia, where the modernist Muslims recognized the advantages of adopting Western methods and techniques in the field of education, science was also incorporated into the curriculum, following its introduction into the Dutch government schools.[23]

A great deal of effort was made in the field of education in the Dutch East Indies by Muhammadiyah. In the spirit of 'Abduh's tradition, the organization has carried out, since its formative years, a massive and multidimensional reformist program in the fields of general and religious education. Thus, influenced to a certain extent by the ideas of 'Abduh and his disciples about equality between men and women, the need for training and educating Muslim girls and women, and improving their social condition in general, Muhammadiyah promoted an ethic of education and training for Muslim girls and women. At the beginning this was done through the women's section of the organization, the 'Aisyiyah, which was founded in 1918 and has been an independent organization since 1923, under the guidance of the Muhammadiyah. Such education, originally initiated to help women understand the meaning of practicing Islam as a way of life and to purify their faith, has been widened along the twentieth-century timeline to include varied educational, social and economic activities, which have had profound effects on the modernization of Indonesian women.[24]

The reformist activities of Muhammadiyah in the field of education had set several targets: making Muslims "better Muslims";[25] reforming and modernizing their lives; spreading Islam among the population; promoting a religious life among the members of Muhammadiyah;[26] promoting the goal of building a Muslim society; and defending Islam against European influence and Christian "attack". The emphasis laid by Muhammadiyah on *tabligh*, as a missionary work for propagating Islam, expresses some of these motivations. The efforts of the Christian missions served as a model for Muhammadiyah's activities in this field.[27]

The efforts made in the field of education for women and girls was initially motivated, to a large extent, by an interest in improving their understanding of Islam and their practice of its precepts as well as enabling them to function properly as housewives and mothers. Much was done in this regard by 'Aisyiyah.[28] In Malaya, besides the call to broaden women's opportunities in the field of education, the *Kaum Muda* advocated greater freedom for women to participate in social affairs.[29]

The Social and Political Dimensions

Although Islamic modernists saw their mission as having primarily religious and educational – not social or political – ends,[30] both the dimensions became deeply grounded in Islamic modernist ideas in the Malay-Indonesian world. Consequently, these two dimensions also became involved in the heated dispute and conflict between the modernists and the traditionalists. The nature of Islam as a total way of life, the comprehensive meaning of the modernist-reformist message, the demand for rapid social change, as well as the inner dynamic of the conflict, caused the reformist message to slide beyond the confines of the strictly religious domain to the social and political dimensions and to involve issues like stratification and power-sharing.

The very tenets of Islamic modernism, and the concept of *ijtihad* in particular, though ostensibly theological in nature, have provocative social–political connotations. They challenged the traditional world-view and its guardians, as they incorporated within themselves a certain defiance toward traditional authorities and social stratification. Thus, even though Islamic modernist spokesmen originally limited themselves to religious reform, especially the purification of worship and ritual and the modernization of religious education, their teachings engenderd far-reaching social and political repercussions. For this same reason, the appellations *Kaum Muda* and *Kaum Tua*, which were originally used to designate Muslim religious modernists and their traditional religious opponents, came to stand for innovators and conservatives in a far wider sense.[31] Deliar Noer argues that *ijtihad* led the modernists to pay regard to opinions rather than to personalities or leaders, and that the modernist teacher (often called *kijahi* or *sjech*) did not enjoy the infallible position of the traditionalist *kijahi*. Similarly, they thought that the modernist teacher had no monopoly on the knowledge of

Islam or any other knowledge, but merely made it available to the public, which has an equal right to discuss it. Therefore, discussions on Islam were not confined to *pesantren* (Islamic schools), *langger* (a small prayer-house) and mosques, but were brought out into the open through newspapers.[32] William Roff, referring to the Malaya of the first four decades of the twentieth century, argues that while the main disputes focused on religious questions, social issues related to them became paramount as a result of social change and the wider implications of the *Kaum Muda* ideas. For Roff, the arguments about whether it was permissible for a Muslim to wear European dress, or to receive interest from post office saving banks, divided people along the same lines as debates regarding the holiness of the local *keramat* (spirit shrine) or whether a teacher had correctly interpreted a verse of the *Qur'an*. In short, he adds, "to be *Kaum Muda* came to mean espousal of modernism in any form; to be *Kaum Tua* was to be in favor of all that was traditional, unchanging and secure".[33]

The wide scope of the *Kaum Muda–Kaum Tua* conflict also manifested itself in the direct defiance of traditional stratification and the division of power, and even in efforts to delegitimize the source of authority of the traditional elite. This was clearly demonstrated in the heated conflict that erupted in the second decade of the twentieth century within the large and influential Hadrami immigrant community in the East Indies. Members of the Hadrami community, who were classified according to the immobile and dominant stratification of their homeland, to the low stratum of *masakin*, or to the middle level of religious leaders, *mashayikh*, began to espouse Islamic modernist perceptions. These perceptions were used by them for changing their social position in their new land. This development is regarded as one of the main manifestations of the "awakening" (*nahdha*) of the Hadrami community in Indonesia during the early years of the twentieth century. A prominent role was played by the Islamic modernist association Jam'iyyat al-Islah wal-Irshad al-'Arabiyya (the Arab Association for Reform and Guidance), established in Batavia (Jakarta) by the Hadramis. Organized in this vital Islamic modernist association, and inspired by Muhammad 'Abduh and Rashid Rida's ideas, many of this community defied traditional stratification and values. In particular, they opposed the privileged position that was assigned in the East Indies to the *sada* (singular: s*ayyid*), who stood at the top of Hadrami society by virtue of their descent from the Prophet Muhammad and their pietism. Thus members of the Hadrami community established basic principles of equality, which were, to a large extent, influenced by Islamic modernist arguments. They argued, among other things, that all Muslim believers enjoy equality before God, that all should have equal rights, and that no man is superior to any other by virtue of his blood. Consequently, the Islamic modernists argued that on principle the *sada* enjoy no privilege in society. Knowing that the *sada* dominated society through the field of education, by shaping private and public opinion, the Hadrami modernists sharply criticized their opponents' monopolized education system as an inferior, stagnant platform for spreading superstitions, and as such, as the source of underdevelopment in Hadrami society. Under the guidance of Jam'iyyat al-Islah wal-Irshad al-'Arabiyya, an educational system was established. This system is considered to be a pivotal aspect of the Hadrami "awakening". It was largely inspired in its philosophy and practice by ideals of Islamic modernism; it also served as a platform for realizing the call for a more flexible and mobile society, by providing the population with proper education and training for modern life. In the long run this educational system proved itself to be a crucial factor in construction of Hadrami identity in Indonesia.[34]

The Islamic modernists challenged the very existence of the traditional order in the Malay-Indonesian world, crossing over from their initial religious arena to social and political spheres. Hence, the attacks of the *Kaum Muda* in Malaya upon established Islam; their ideas were regarded as attacks upon the traditional elite, which stood behind, and was involved with, the religious hierarchy. Athough *Kaum Muda*'s criticism of *adat* was limited to its detrimental effects on the practice of Islam, or was linked to their insistence upon the equality of all men before God, both critiques could be regarded as having subversive implications for the existing social and political, as well as the religious, order.[35] Shanti Nair writes that Islamic modernism, as it was articulated by the *Kaum Muda*, challenged the traditional religious authority that was located in the village-based *'ulama*, scholars and functionaries to the sultans, who were largely constituted by the *Kaum Tua* movement, "whose ideals rested in the preservation of the Malay elites and of the royal courts".[36]

At an early stage of the Islamic modernist movement in the Malay-Indonesian world, the Islamic modernist journal *al-Imam* dared to decry the traditional Malay rulers, the sultans (or the rajas), who constituted the focus of political authority in traditional Malay society. The journal did not limit itself to the Malay peninsula, but was also a platform for criticizing traditional rulers in the Indonesian archipelago as well. Opposing the Malay rulers, the journal even challenged their divine power and authority that was rationalized and legitimized in Islamic terms, and the whole royal ideology, *kerajaan*. In its bold defiance of the ruling elite in the peninsular states (the sultanates), *al-Imam* benefited from the liberal climate in Singapore, a British-governed enclave, as well as the fact that the city-state was beyond the reach of the sultanates. The Malay rulers, the *rajas*, were criticized by the journal, inter alia, for not enforcing the Islamic law, *shari'a*, and even disobeying it. They were also censured for their failure to respond to the European challenge, for neglecting the welfare of the Malay community, and for their injustice. In brief, they were denounced as the source of all the ills this community suffered from. The lifestyle of the court elites was also criticized. The titles and ceremony of the *kerajaan*, for example, were rejected as being frivolous, and the emphasis on luxurious display was condemned. The whole basis of the *kerajaan* was even brought into question by *al-Imam*, including the basic position of the sultan (raja) as the focus of loyalty and the symbol of Muslim unity. Islam, not the sultans and royal allegiance, were presented as the focus of the Islamic community, called the *umat* (Arabic: *umma*). The divine law of God, *shari'a*, not the royal court, was presented as the ideal legitimate basis of the community. *Al-Imam*'s arguments implied that the *'ulama*, not the rajas, should guide the *umat* by being influential in all aspects of Muslim community life and preparing for the challenge of the new world. By using the term *umat* for Malay society, *al-Imam* actually rejected the ideological basis of the traditional collective identity, *kerajaan*, and implicitly granted a secondary significance to a collective identity based on the Malay race, *bangsa*.[37]

From the 1910s, Islamic modernist ideas began to spread into the domain of political parties; consequently the conflict between the *Kaum Muda* and *Kaum Tua* also extended into the political sphere. But the essential politicization of the image of the *Kaum Muda*, according to William Roff, began to make itself evident only in the mid-1920s with the involvement of Islamic modernists in the conflict in the Malay-Indonesian world about the collective identity of the political communities.[38]

The intellectual discourse among Islamic modernists in the Malay-Indonesian world in the 1920s about the issue of collective identity was manifested primarily in two modernist-oriented journals published by Indonesian and Malay students at the University of al-Azhar in Cairo: *Seruan Azhar* ("Call of al-Azhar"), published 1925–8, and *Pilihan Timur* ("Choice of the East"), published 1927–8. These two journals, which were banned by the Dutch in Indonesia but were freely available in the Straits Settlements, were involved in an overt political discussion that included the expression of pan-Islamic ideas and expectations. This discussion was largely influenced by the contemporary political activity in Egypt pertaining to the Caliphate question, which followed the abolition of the Caliphate in 1924. The two journals were also used as a stage for the expression of support for the idea of pan-Malayanism (union between Indonesia and Malaya), as well as for anti-colonial nationalism. Cairo, particularly in the 1920s, also provided a fertile ground for students from the Malay-Indonesian world to freely express their political sentiments and anti-colonial sentiments in particular.[39]

The Islamic modernists contributed to the development of a national identity in both Dutch East India and Malaya. In the former they worked, at a preliminary stage, to foster collective ideas and sentiments beyond diversified ethnic origins, playing the role of "pre-nationalism",[40] establishing a "proto-nationalist movement",[41] and adapting a variation on anti-colonial attitude.[42] In Malaya they even created an interesting conceptual linkage between Islam and nationalism by introducing the concept of a universal Muslim community, the *umma*, into the debate about Malay nationalism. In this manner, the Islamic modernists strengthened the equation that had pre-colonial roots between the Malay ethnic element in the national identity and the Muslim religious element. Through this conceptual approach, they also established the first linkage between religion and politics in the earliest forms of Malay nationalism.[43] Hence, contrary to the intense struggle in the history of many Muslim societies between nationalism and Islam, Malay nationalism, in its earliest articulation, combined Malay nationalist and Islamic ideals. Historically, argues Shanti Nair, Malay nationalism reflected "an ethnic assertiveness incorporating religious identity".[44]

This process of politicization of the Islamic modernists in the Dutch East Indies also took place out of their need to confront other world-views and ideologies in the early twentieth century. Prominent among these was Communism. The modernists' rivalry with this ideology was confined to the 1920s.[45] Another competing ideology was Javanism, as a Javanist separatist idea, or nationalism of a Javanese character, which inevitably contradicted the idea of establishing Islam as a collective bond of unity.[46] But by far the most serious conflict that the Islamic modernists participated in was in the clash between Islam and "secular"[47] nationalism. This debate, which reached its height in the 1920s and the 1930s, saw the "secularists," prominent among them the Dutch-educated Indonesians, propose a type of nationalism, *kebangsaan*. They called for a joint collective identity outside the context of Islam that comprised all the people of Indonesia, irrespective of faith and ethnic origin. Their message seriously defied Islam by questioning the justifiability of various Islamic teachings and institutions, such as the pilgrimage to Mecca and polygamy, and by disparaging the benefits of its services and rituals as obstacles to progress. The *kebangsaan* was viewed by Islamic modernists, among others, as a kind of new religion.[48] This conflict was a preliminary stage in regard to a significant and lasting issue in the political–ideological debate that has taken place in Indonesia since the 1940s between Islam and the state, also known as the issue of *umat* and *negara*. It was epitomized in the 1945 debate about the "philosophical basis" for an independent Indonesia and the prolonged discourse about the meaning and interpretation of *Pancasila*, the Indonesian state ideology.

The extension of the Islamic modernist ideology to the political sphere as an expression of the unity between religion and politics embodied in the Great Tradition of Islam, the Islamic orthodox tradition which has a legal nature, was also regarded with anxiety by the Dutch colonial regime in the East Indies. It was deeply concerned about the militant and political aspects of Islam, observing them according to its revised policy toward Islam in the East Indies. This policy was based on the guidelines drawn up at the end of the nineteenth century by "the architect of Netherlands Islamic policy in the Indies", Christian Snouck Hurgronje.[49] Snouck Hurgronje was a distinguished Dutch scholar and an expert in Islam: in the late 1800s he was nominated as an adviser of Islamic affairs to the Dutch colonial government, formally, the Adviser on Arabian and Native Affairs. Snouck Hurgronje was relatively moderate in his attitude toward Islam. The major guidelines of his policy postulated toleration of the Muslim faith, combined with vigilance toward Islamic, especially pan-Islamic, political activities. These guidelines continued to characterize the policy of the Dutch colonial administration even after the appearance of Islamic modernism in the Dutch East Indies and the rapid growth of Muslim activism that threatened "to blur the thin and artificial dividing line between the religiously tolerable and the politically intolerable".[50] Nevertheless, suspicious of the potential political threat embodied in Islamic modernism and guided by a policy of divide and rule, the Dutch government officials tried to obstruct and suppress the spread of Islamic modernism in the East Indies. Therefore, traditional indigenous rulers like *priyayi* (Javanese administrative upper classes) and *adat* chiefs, who regarded the Islamic modernist leaders as their rivals, were favored by the Dutch, and traditionalist Muslims, who were concerned mainly with purely religious questions, also enjoyed a more preferred position.[51]

In the Malay states, in contrast to the Dutch East Indies and the Straits Settlements, the consolidating unity between Islam and politics was less influential. This is due largely to the British colonial policy in the Malay states, which differed from the policy applied by the British in the Straits Settlements. British colonial policy in the Malay states favored and subsequently strengthened all the traditional elements of Malay society, as well as the traditional rulers and elites. Hence, the British encouraged the concentration of doctrinal and administrative religious authority in the hands of the apparatus dependent on the sultans. This policy also promoted economic modernization, whose major impact was on the non-Muslim immigrant groups. Therefore, social change among the Muslim community was relatively limited and the traditional social linkages of the rural Malay community were scarcely dislocated. Another result of British colonial policy in Malaya was to play down the relevance of "high" Islamic culture to the Malay community on the one hand, and to play up the folklore of the "real Malay" on the other hand.[52] British colonial rule in the Malaya peninsula was considerably less concerned than the Dutch with Islamic militancy and pan-Islamism. This was partly due to the absence of an organized class of *'ulama* in Malaya as well as the absence of a strong tradition of *'ulama* opposition to the authorities, such as did exist in Sumatra and Java.[53] Consequently the British colonial regime in the Malay peninsula made no attempt to restrict the Muslims' pilgrimage, as was done by Dutch colonial rule in the East Indies in the nineteenth century, where the *hajji*s were viewed as a source of potentially serious unrest. British Malaya policy may also partly explain the relatively liberal attitude of the British toward Islamic modernist activity in the Straits Settlements.[54]

Challenging the Traditional World

In the 1920s and 1930s the Islamic modernist movement in the Dutch East Indies was also involved in a conflict with secular ideologies, which would become more crucial in the post-colonial period when the formulation of the collective identity of the Indonesian political community moved to the center of the political stage. But in the period under discussion, the first decades of the twentieth century, the conflict between the Islamic modernists and the Islamic traditionalists, known as the *Kaum Muda–Kaum Tua* conflict, was much more pronounced. In the 1930s the bitterness and heat of this conflict slowly began to dissipate, for several reasons. A rapprochement in the Dutch East Indies, between the modernists and the Islamic traditionalists and conservatives in the 1930s, partly resulted from changes and reforms introduced by the traditionalists, including the adoption of certain modernist ideas and activities, such as the modernizing of schools. The moderation of the conflict was also a result of a mutual realization on both sides that, despite the differences of opinion regarding certain religious ideas and practices, their basic creed remained the same. The traditionalists also began to share the modernists' concerns regarding the Dutch encroachment in the realm of religion.[55] As for Malaya, the moderation of the *Kaum Muda–Kaum Tua* conflict is explained, among other things, by the fact that Islamic modernists in Malaya drew closer to the Islamic traditionalists as a result of the common situation in which they found themselves, i.e. the threat of secular nationalism, as well as the improved standards of religious education and the demise of an older generation.[56]

The Islamic modernist ideology in the Malay-Indonesian world was primarily a challenge to the traditional status quo. Islamic modernism brought about a deep cultural conflict between fundamentally conflicting doctrines, ideas, practices, values, and institutions: *ijtihad* versus *taqlid*; Islam and *shari'a* versus *adat*; modern *madrasa* versus traditional religious training and teaching systems. This conflict can be also depicted in terms of dichotomy: religious modernism and reformism versus traditionalism; orthodoxy, "pure" faith (or purism) and Scripturalism versus heresy, heterodoxy, syncretism and mysticism; Great Tradition versus Little Tradition; universal religion versus local custom; urban Islam versus rural Islam; and "high culture" versus popular or folk culture.

Due to the multi-dimensional nature of the challenge posed by Islamic modernism, it is not surprising that the conflict between the Islamic modernists and their opponents became so intense. Neither does it come as a surprise that Islamic modernism in the Malay-Indonesian world, essentially an urban-centered phenomenon, aroused the opposition of considerable elements in the traditional elites, the upholders of status quo who included: traditional and rural *'ulama*; the official religious hierarchy in Malaya;[57] the custodians and guardians of *adat,* the *adat* chiefs, or *adat* functionaries; religious teachers; leaders of Sufi orders; and traditional rulers. A clear response on the organizational level of the traditionalists to the modernist challenge was the establishment in 1926 in Java, by traditional *'ulama*, of the Nahdlatul Ulama (NU) organization. It should be noted that the NU was the first modern-style organization of the traditionalists, copying some of the modernists' innovations in regard to its structure and activity.[58]

A Comparative Look at Egypt

Taking a comparative look at Egypt provides further insights and a more comprehensive view about Islamic modernism in the Malay-Indonesian world. The role played by the transmission of Islamic modernist ideas from Egypt was crucial in laying down the conceptual basis of the Islamic modernist movement in the Malay-Indonesian world.

The Islamic modernist movement, significantly influenced by 'Abduh's heritage, made a strong, vivid impact in the Malay-Indonesian world early on. In contrast, in Egypt 'Abduh's heritage dissolved quite early on into various and contradicting conceptual trends, ideologies, and movements. Its elements were to be found almost everywhere in Egypt in the first decades of the twentieth century, and were echoed in almost every ideological and intellectual discourse, debate, and conflict that took place at the time in Egypt. Prominent among these conflicts were those that resembled the major cultural and ideological debates going on in the Malay-Indonesian world, such as modernity versus tradition, and the determination of the collective national identity. But at the same time 'Abduh's heritage, with many of its authentic characteristics, did not exist there as a solid, vivid corpus of ideas, and definitely not as a formidable organizational reality, as the Muhammadiyah organization has been in Indonesia.

During his lifetime, Muhammad 'Abduh faced fierce opposition to his reformist ideas, projects, and activities that were mainly connected to his positions as chairman of the Committee of the Administration of al-Azhar, the Mufti of Egypt, member of the Superior Council of the *Awqaf* Administration, and member of the Legislative Assembly. A high degree of antagonism was expressed by the conservatives. The *'ulama* within al-Azhar were among the leaders of this opposition. They were apprehensive about the significance that 'Abduh attributed to reforming and modernizing al-Azhar, the stronghold of Islamic sciences, as an imperative step in reforming Islam throughout the Islamic world. Part of the opposition to 'Abduh was more a reflection of political interests and considerations than an expression of a conservative world-view per se. Indeed, there were some in al-Azhar, and many more outside it, who favored 'Abduh's ideas and activities, but avoided expressing their position publicly. Thus, the boldness and decisiveness of 'Abduh's opponents and, in contrast, the weakness of his sympathizers, as well as the fact that the ruler of Egypt, the Khedieve 'Abbas II, switched from a favorable attitude to 'Abduh's ideas to a determined opposition to his proposed reforms, frustrated many of his efforts to put his reformist ideas into practice.[59]

But in comparison to the extent of the threat to the essentials of traditional society revealed in 'Abduh's heritage in the Malay-Indonesian world, the concrete challenge posed by 'Abduh in his own lifetime to the traditional society of Egypt was limited, cautious in its approach, and less provocative in its implications. For this reason, the reaction in Egypt to 'Abduh's reformist ideas, projects, and activities did not develop into a deep cultural conflict as expressed in the *Kaum Muda–Kaum Tua* conflict. Similarly, Islamic modernism, per se, did not express itself explicitly and directly in the bitter cultural, conceptual, and literary debate that took place in Egypt between tradition and change in the first decades of the twentieth century. The conflict between the "old" (*al-qadim*) and the "new" (*al-jadid*), or between the "old school" (*al-Madrasa al-Qadima*) and the "modernist school" (*al-Madrasa al-Haditha*), which reached its zenith between World Wars I and II, was a noticeable characteristic of Egypt's history during that period of time.[60] Thus, whilst the conflict between the *Kaum Muda* and the *Kaum Tua* was almost entirely connected with Islamic modernism as a solid ideology, which clearly manifested itself in organizational structures, in the conflict between the "new" and the "old," in Egypt, Islamic modernism seems to be an amorphous and intangible entity, an inspiring heritage that dissolved into varied conceptual directions and world-views. The "sounds" of Islamic modernism in Egypt *did* echo everywhere through the conflict between the "new" and the "old" and in almost every issue, serving many individuals, groups, and organizations who used them eclectically. 'Abduh's heirs, argues Malcolm H. Kerr, "were, of course, the product of various other influences as well, which sometimes combined with the ambiguity of 'Abduh's legacy to promote additional tensions and equivocations of their own".[61] Hence, 'Abduh's thought was doomed, in the intensive conceptual and ideological climate of its birth-place, to pass through channels that obscured and even distorted its essentials, making it almost impossible to evaluate its influence.

However, bearing in mind the marked movement of 'Abduh's heritage in Egypt toward *salafi* positions since the end of the 1920s, it might be assumed that Islamic modernism in the Malay-Indonesian world could also not avoid the *salafi* influence. Such an assumption derives from the fact that Rashid Rida's Egyptian *al-Manar* was a significant channel for transmitting modernist ideas from Egypt to the Malay-Indonesian world throughout the creation of the Islamic modernist movement there, even though 'Abduh's authentic heritage also appears to have substantially underpinned the conceptual basis of the Islamic modernist movement in the Malay-Indonesian world. It must be noted that from a later historical perspective, beyond the boundaries of the formative period and into recent decades, Muhammadiyah, in Indonesia, is alleged to show more of a link with Rashid Rida's *salafism* than with the modernist ideas of 'Abduh, and has adopted a position of "neo-*salafism*", including an ideological emphasis on a return to pristine Islam and strict Scripturalism.[62]

Historical Role and Impacts

The Islamic modernist school of thought in the Malay-Indonesian world strongly challenged the domestic traditional order early in the twentieth century, inflaming a substantial confrontation between orthodox Islam and syncretic religion, between "high culture" and popular culture, between a global type of Islam and local Islam and between the *shari'a* and the *adat*. The implications of this bitter confrontation transcended the Islamic religious sphere, to include educational, social, and political aspects.

It is striking how the followers of Islamic modernism in the Malay-Indonesian world, chiefly in Indonesia, then the Dutch East Indies, the Straits Settlements and to a lesser extent, Malaya, succeeded in establishing a significant movement. Present-day Indonesia is the only place in all of Southeast Asia where Islamic modernism remains "a major, organized force".[63] The Muhammadiyah organization, which has a highly significant position in the narrative of Islamic modernism in Indonesia, now claims about 30 million members. This organization was described at the end of the 1970s as "the most powerful living reformist movement in Muslim Southeast Asia, perhaps in the entire Muslim culture".[64] The vitality and energy of the Islamic modernist movement in Indonesia has contributed substantially to the fact that in Indonesia, the orthodox Muslims are largely divided between the modernists and the traditionalists. In Malaysia, in contrast, the country with the second largest Muslim population in Southeast Asia, where there is a high level of homogeneity within the Islamic population, and the vast majority of Muslims are traditionalists,[65] Islamic modernist thought is represented by "a small number of thinkers in the 'Abduh-Afghani tradition".[66] This can be historically explained by the fact that the early Islamic modernist movement in Malaya was much less widespread and influential than in the Dutch East Indies.

The greatest success of the Islamic modernist movement in the Malay-Indonesian world was to take the ideas borrowed from Egypt far beyond their original boundaries. They made 'Abduh's ideas, essentially religious in their character, a platform for an original and comprehensive reformist project that posed a substantial challenge to the traditional status quo. The modernists in the Malay-Indonesian world therefore also played a modernizing role, including adapting the transmitted ideas to their own locality and particular conditions, and making them a basis for their own intellectual creativity. The modernists were also successful in maintaining the authentic and formative ideas and ideals of Islamic modernism. Indeed, it can be argued that in recent years Islamic modernism in Indonesia has moved from its preliminary progressive and reformist spirit, losing much of its intellectual momentum. However, the original voice of Muhammad 'Abduh still persists in the modernist Islamic movement in Indonesia, even inspiring influential circles in the Islamic mainstream. Significant in this regard is the case of neo-modernism (known also as Islamic liberalism) in Indonesia. Muhammad 'Abduh's heritage appears to be a significant source of inspiration of progressive ideas in the Islamic context for neo-modernism, which emerged in the early 1970s to become an influential stream of thought in Islamic discourse in Indonesia; this will be further discussed below.

Espousing purism and Scripturalism, Islamic modernism in the Malay-Indonesian world also strengthened the religious and cultural position of the Great Tradition in the regional Islamic mosaic. Consequently, the Islamic modernist movement in the Malay-Indonesian world has strengthened the conceptual centrality of *shari'a* among Muslims in Indonesia. In this sense the Islamic modernist movement in the Malay-Indonesian world is likely to facilitate religious and intellectual interaction between the "center" of the Muslim world and the Indonesian-Malay world.

Another prominent role played by Islamic modernism in the Malay-Indonesian world was that of agents of social change and modernization among its followers.[67] Notable in this context are the substantial and intensive efforts made in the field of educational reform, including promoting women's opportunities in the education system and employment. These efforts designated social modernization as one of the main tenets of Islamic modernizm's activity in the Malay-Indonesian world.

In Egypt, in contrast, Islamic modernist stream of thought has, as described earlier, been diluted and transmogrified into disparate sets of values and ideologies. As Malcolm H. Kerr relates:

> Such diverse individuals as the liberal constitutionalist Ahmad Lutfi as-Sayyid, the militant fundamentalist Hasan al-Bana of the Muslim Brethren, and Gamal 'Abd an-Nasir can all be identified, each in a different way, as heirs of 'Abduh. 'Abduh's historical role was simply to fling open the doors and expose a musty tradition to fresh currents. His intention may have been more specific, but the effect was not..[68]

Islamic Modernism in the Malay-Indonesian World: Suggested Explanations

Although it defied the traditional values, cultural codes, and institutions of mainstream Indonesian culture and society, Islamic modernism was able to adapt and not only survive, but flourish. The following factors may explain this phenomenon: a pluralist religious context; historically, clever cultural "borrowing"; the existence of a developed organizational basis; the creative adaptation of modernist ideas into varied fields of activity; the maintaining of a low political profile.

Robert W. Hefner claims that the most unusual feature and distinctive quality of Islam in Southeast Asia, in particular of Indonesian Islam, has long been its remarkable and established tradition of intellectual and organizational pluralism. Relative to many other Muslim countries, many prominent Indonesian Muslim leaders support the pluralistic understanding of religion. Even in pre-modern times neither the courts nor the *'ulama* exercised an effective monopoly of power over the moral and intellectual life of the Muslim community in the Malay-Indonesian world. There were diverse alternative ideas and religious views as well as multiple ways concerning how to be a good Muslim. From the beginning, the people of the archipelago, says Hefner, grappled with what social theorists today often regard as a uniquely modern issue, namely, cultural pluralism.[69] It is likely that the absence, more in Indonesia than in Malaya, of a strong central Islamic establishment, similar to that of al-Azhar in Egypt, as well as the existence of a basic pluralism, gave the Islamic modernists more room to maneuver in the Malay-Indonesian world, and also provided them with an imperative precondition for their survival in the Muslim community there.

Another explanation for Islamic modernism's thriving may be found in the transmission of Islamic modernist ideas from Egypt to the Dutch East Indies and the Malay peninsula. Perhaps the large-scale transmission of ideas – via a complex cross-regional cultural network of cultural brokers and intellectual institutions – and their transplantation in the Malay-Indonesian world, have been more than a random imitation of fashionable ideas, or the unavoidable traffic of thought from the "center" of Islamic world to its "periphery". This transmission of ideas may, rather, express a clever, intuitive historical selection. In the face of the threatening clash between tradition and modernity, and the collective early twentieth-century mood of weakness in the entire Islamic world, many in the Muslim community in the Malay-Indonesian world were receptive to the conceptual heritage that emerged in Egypt toward the end of the nineteenth century, when the Muslim community there found itself in a similar historical predicament. Witnessing confusion, weakness, and the sense of being threatened.

Muhammad 'Abduh, who followed the aspirations of his teacher and colleague Jamal al-Din al-Afghani, hoped to propose a comprehensive reformist doctrine to the Muslim community in Egypt and to the *umma* in general. Since they were alert to all the activity in the "center" of the Muslim world, many Muslim communities in the Malay-Indonesian world adapted this doctrine in a way marked by conceptual confidence, diligence, and creativity.

On a more practical level, the historical accomplishments of Islamic modernism in Indonesia throughout the twentieth century are closely linked to the existence of Muhammadiyah. The fact that Muhammadiyah has never been a political organization nor directly involved in politics (even though, inevitably, it has been unable to totally avoid political involvement), largely contributed to its room for maneuver. This formally apolitical stance enabled the organization to avoid taking a radical political position against Dutch colonial rule.[70]

The varied roles played by the Islamic modernist movement in the Malay-Indonesian world may also explain its survival and vitality. By being active in varied spheres of life and fulfilling multidimensional historical missions, the Islamic modernist movement in the Malay-Indonesian world seems to have adopted a survivor's strategy in the sense of a broad *raison d'être* and a relatively wide range of alternative courses of action.

The Islamic modernist school of thought in the Malay-Indonesian world strongly challenged the domestic traditional order early in the twentieth century, inflaming a substantial confrontation between orthodox Islam and syncretic religion, between "high culture" and popular culture, between a global type of Islam and local Islam and between the *shari'a* and the *adat*. The implications of this bitter confrontation transcended the Islamic religious sphere, to include educational, social, and political aspects.

Primarily, the powerful challenge that was posed by the Islamic modernist movement in the Malay-Indonesian world to the entire traditional order is revealed by comparing it to the function played by Islamic modernist stream of thought in Egypt. The same can be said about the historical role played by Islamic modernism in the Malay-Indonesian world: its multidimensional nature becomes much clearer and self-evident when looks at Egypt in comparison.

A decisive impact of the local context on the historical course of development of Muhammad 'Abduh's heritage in the Malay-Indonesia world has also become more evident by using a comparative view. Disseminated from the Middle East, the ideas of Islamic modermism have been developed in their "new home" in the Malay-Indonesian world, the Indonesia archipelago in particular, to a vivid, challenging and influential movement, whereas in the Middle East 'Abduh's Islamic modernist heritage did not develop into a substantial movement, dissolving quite early on into various and contradicting conceptual trends and movements. Considering the development of Islamic modernist ideas into a massive movement in Indonesia one must question the claim that 'Abduh's conceptual heritage contains within itself an intrinsic ambivalence and ambiguity, and that therefore it was predestined to be absorbed into more assertive ideologies, as occurred in Egypt.

2

Radical Islamic Fundamentalism in Indonesia

Global and Local Contexts

Fundamentalism has historical antecedents, but no ideological precursors.

(Bruce B. Lawrence)

Current analysis of the "Islamic space" in Indonesia cannot ignore radical Islamic fundamentalism taking shape there. Various developments and occurrences have served to heighten suspicions and anxieties regarding this multi-dimensional phenomenon in the Indonesian archipelago. Conspicuous among them are the growing manifestations and impact of radical Islamic activity in Indonesia over the past few years, in particular the Bali bombings on October 12, 2002, and the global wake-up call, stirred by the threatening effects of September 11. The result has meant increasing attention given by the media to Islamic radicalism and militancy in Southeast Asia, and in Indonesia in particular.

There is a growing tendency in recent years to consider radical Islamic fundamentalism in Indonesia as a local case of a much broader, global, phenomenon. This chapter aims to examine the nature of the globalized dimension radical Islamic fundamentalism in Indonesia by focusing mainly on its significant conceptual aspects, including the issue of transmission of radical Islamic ideas from the Middle East to Indonesia. This will be done by addressing both the current perspective and the broader historical perspective; the two perspectives will complement each other in order to create an enhanced view of radical Islamic fundamentalism in Indonesia.

Radical Islamic Fundamentalism

Ideology and Perception

Fundamentalism is considered to be a sort of religious ideology. Certain general characteristics join together to form the ideological contours of Islamic fundamentalism, including its radical expression. Groups, organizations, and movements in Indonesia, however, which can be included to varying degrees in the definition of radical fundamentalism, or under similar definitions such as radical Islam, radical Islamism and so on, are not a homogeneous entity. As with radical Muslims elsewhere, radical Muslims in Indonesia are split organizationally and divided among themselves over several issues. Indeed, some essential fundamentalist perceptions are also espoused by parties based on Islamic political agendas, unlike the "pluralist Islamic parties" which accept the secular-oriented state ideology, *Pancasila*, as a sole or joint basis, whilst at the same time using some Islamic symbols.[1]

The former type of Islamic political party, which emerged during the process of a mushrooming of political parties that succeeded the fall of Suharto in May 1998, have adopted an accommodative political approach, aiming to achieve their Islamic ideological goals through democratic political action as legitimate political actors. This type of political party is therefore not included in this book in the category of radical Islamic fundamentalism. It must be noted that their accommodating approach has been explicitly denounced by some radical fundamentalists in Indonesia,[2] just as in the Middle East. Partai Keadilan Sejahtera (PKS, Prosperous Justice Party), formerly named Partai Keadilan (PK, Justice Party), is an interesting example of that type of party; it was originally inspired by the Muslim Brotherhood in Egypt but in its later, non-violent and compromising phase, there is no longer any trace of its old radical and militant strategy. The success of the PKS in the parliamentary elections of April 2004 is impressive – about 7.2 percent of the vote; as

Partai Keadilan it won only about 1.4 percent in 1999. The fact that PKS campaigned strongly on significant universal issues – such as opposing corruption and graft, combating injustice and building a strong image of a clean politics, while playing down its support for the introduction of the *shari'a* and avoiding an explicit campaign to promote an Islamic state – helped the party in the polls.[3]

A cluster of ideological perceptions and attitudes have emerged that have enabled analysts to portray radical fundamentalism in the Islamic world by bridging conceptual nuances and a diversity of organizational behavior and strategies. The same is applicable to the case of radical fundamentalists in Indonesia. Primarily, the radical fundamentalists in Indonesia share the essential notion of the Islamic fundamentalists of establishing an Islamic state based on *shari'a*, the Islamic law. This feature is the driving power of radical Muslims worldwide, eager to see the establishment of the authority of God (*al-hakimiyya*). As to the boundaries of the desired Islamic state, several models can be identified in Indonesia. Rather noticeably, there is an ancient call to establish an Indonesian Islamic state per se. Jama'ah Islamiyah is said to espouse the idea of an Islamic state to include Indonesia, Malaysia, Singapore, Southern Thailand, and the Southern Philippines. The organizational activity of Jama'ah Islamiyah and its alleged antecedent, Pondok Ngruki, also known as the "Ngruki Network", spilled out of Indonesia to cover in its activity Singapore, Malaysia, and even the Southern Philippines.[4] This has brought with it the idea of establishing an international caliphate – an idea clearly presented at the Mujahidin Congress held in Yogyakarta in August 2000. Perhaps this concept has been borrowed from the Hizb al-Tahrir al-Islami (Islamic Liberation Party).[5] This radical Islamic movement was established in Jerusalem in 1952/3 by Palestinian religious functionaries, who had broken away from the Muslim Brothers. In its formative years the movement was based mainly in the West Bank. Gradually it has extended its activity throughout the Middle East and beyond. Today, Hizb al-Tahrir al-Islami has a branch in Indonesia, known as Hizbut Tahrir, and it is vocal among radical Muslims.[6] By placing the idea of establishing an Islamic state as a conceptual pivot of their world-view, radical fundamentalists in Indonesia share the unequivocal assertion that legitimate sovereignty belongs to God and that consequently political order is considered to be an expression on earth of the will of God and its rule on earth.

The idea of the implementation of *shari'a*, which is also an essential component of the world-view of radical fundamentalists in Indonesia, is tightly connected in fundamentalist perceptions with the call for an Islamic state. Since a regime can exercise sovereignty only in the name of God, *shari'a*, the Divine Law, provides the inspiring principles. The legitimacy of authority is deeply conditioned by strict adherence to *shari'a*. It has to be the sole source of law and to supply the norms and codes of behavior for the *umma*, the community of believers. This pivotal claim attests to the holistic nature of Islam. The religious, legal, and political spheres are closely integrated in the world-view of fundamentalists in the Islamic world; autonomous political space is entirely rejected on the grounds that Islam provides knowledge about every aspect of life. The idea of separation between the transcendental and the temporal, and consequently between religion and the state, is denied.[7] The existing political system in Indonesia, based on the secular-oriented state ideology, *Pancasila*, is also rejected by many who hold Islamic fundamentalist perceptions in Indonesia, let alone the zealous radical fundamentalists themselves. There are those who even reject the national symbol of the state by refusing to fly the Indonesian flag.[8] Whereas radical fundamentalists call for implementation of s*hari'a*, Indonesian Muslims who hold "soft" fundamentalist perceptions agree, at least as a transitional stage, to see constitutional recognition of the Jakarta Charter from 1945: the original preamble to the constitution, from which were removed, at the last moment, seven words that required Muslims to observe *shari'a*.[9]

Side by side with the ultimate goal of establishing an Islamic state based on *shari'a*, radical fundamentalists in Indonesia, as with radical fundamentalists elsewhere in the Islamic world, profoundly espouse the obligation of *jihad*. Within an Islamic juridical–theological view, the concept of *jihad* embodies one's duty to exert efforts along God's path, by spreading the belief in God and making His word supreme over this world. This includes turning all people into Muslim believers. The concept of *jihad*, in this sense, is a broad one and is not limited to an act of war or physical fighting. The obligation of *jihad* can be fulfilled either by heart, tongue, hands, or sword.[10] In other words, it can be achieved by both peaceful and violent means. From the point of view of radical fundamentalists in the Islamic world, *jihad* is required in order to remove obstacles placed in the way of establishing the authority of God, and all kinds of efforts are needed: a comprehensive *jihad* must therefore be carried out. It may include violent or military *jihad*,[11] known, among other things, as *jihad bil-saif* ("striving through the sword"), either in order to defend Islam if needed, or to expand it. In a similar way to radical Islamic fundamentalism in the Islamic world, radical fundamentalists in Indonesia address, in the name of *jihad*, both sheer acts of violence and terror and non-violent actions. A military manifestation of *jihad*, in a sense of Holy War, was demonstrated to a large extent by the Laskar Jihad movement, the largest and best organized Muslim militia in Indonesia, until it declared its disbanding soon after the Bali bombings on October 12, 2002. Laskar Jihad was formally established in January 2000 in Yogyakarta, as a direct response to the violent conflict in Maluku between Christians and Muslims. In an urgent attempt to defeat the Christians in Maluku, in April–May 2000, Laskar Jihad shipped several thousands of its fighters to Maluku. The Laskar Jihad military involvement, which has strongly aggravated the conflict there, was carried out under the Islamic war cry of *jihad,* portraying the Christian community as a contemporary embodiment of medieval crusaders.[12] The movement even claimed to receive seven *fatwa*s (legal opinions) issued by seven different *salafi* muftis, six of them in Saudi Arabia and one in Yemen, generally justifying Muslim actions in Maluku on the basis of Muslims being allegedly attacked by Christians. It was on the basis of these *fatwas* that Ja'far Umar Talib, the leader of Laskar Jihad, declared *jihad* against the Christians of Maluku, presenting it as a compulsory duty in response to the attack of the Christian "enemies" on the Muslims.[13] Indeed, the concept of *jihad* was radicalized in the rhetoric of Laskar Jihad and emphasis was placed on the military aspect of this concept within the activities of the organization, which was deeply involved in the military conflict in Maluku. Still, Laskar Jihad seemed to share the understanding that *jihad* is a comprehensive concept, and as such is not limited to an act of war.[14]

There are a number of activities of radical Muslims in Indonesia that can be included in the category of propagation of Islam and religious proselytization. This is known in the Malay-Indonesian world as *dakwah* (Arabic: *da'wa*), and it includes strengthening the faith of Muslims who have become lax in their beliefs. It is true that this kind of activity is carried out not only by radical Muslims but it is primarily they who are extremely zealous in the *da'wa* activity. They hold it to be a significant duty, side by side with the militant aspect of *jihad*, for the transformation of Muslim society at large, which they see as living in injustice and ignorance of the true way of Islam, to be transformed into a genuine Islamic society and polity.[15] Laskar Jihad portrayed its *jihad* against the Christians in Maluku as a form of *da'wa* aimed at building an ideal Islamic society. They even demonstrated the integration between *jihad* and *da'wa* by establishing a civilian infrastructure for local Muslims.[16] Clearly, this attitude of the Laskar Jihad also attests to its understanding of the *jihad* as multifaceted.

There is also a wide range of activities carried out by radical fundamentalists in Indonesia that are portrayed as "anti-vice" campaigns.[17] This category includes, among other things, campaigns against "places of sin", such as raiding nightclubs, gambling centers, bars, discothèques, and casinos. It also includes imposing Islamic moral values on men and women, and demands the closing of entertainment centers during the month of Ramadan. Similar activities are also known among radical Muslims elsewhere. This kind of activity can also be included in the general concept of *da'wa*.

Radical fundamentalists need worthy adversaries. Confrontation and opposition are essential to their vitality, for clearly demarcating the borders between them and the unbelievers, to prevent contamination and to maintain purity. Therefore the *takfir*, excommunication of an individual from the *umma*, is important for radical fundamentalists who consider themselves to be the "true Muslims".[18] The *takfir* is also a crucial element in the conceptual heritage of their ideological forefather, the Egyptian Sayyid Qutb (1906–66), the radical thinker of the Muslim Brothers. The rhetoric and behavior of radical fundamentalists in the Islamic world attests to the importance they pay to the *takfir*. Fundamentalists, no matter what religious context they are located in, tend to generate their own vocabulary.[19] It is not surprising, therefore, that in the vocabulary of radical Muslims the terms *kafir* (unbeliever, infidel) and *kufur* (unbelief, infidelity) take significant hold side by side with the concepts of *shari'a* and *jihad*. Radical fundamentalists in Indonesia share the ideology of other Muslims in this aspect, being urged to identify unbelievers, to be wary of them, and to defeat them in due course. Laskar Jihad, confronting the "infidels" in Maluku, gave a great deal of attention to the issue of the "enemies" of Islam in general, and to the concept of *kafir* in particular.[20] This may partly be explained by the fact that Ja'far Umar Thalib, the head of Laskar Jihad, who spent two years fighting with the Afghan *mujahidin* against the Soviet forces, supported a strict *salafi* faction among the *mujahidin*, who placed particular emphasis on the concept of *takfir*.[21]

The basic vigilance and animosity of radical fundamentalists toward the "infidels" is also embodied in the concept of "new *jahiliyya*", or "modern *jahiliyya*". Originally the term *jahiliyya* referred to the ignorance and godlessness that prevailed in pre-Islamic Arabia. The concept of "new *jahiliyya*" is a reactualization of the original term and is connected with Sayyid Qutb and the Pakistani theologian Abul-A'la al-Mawdudi (1903–79). Al-Mawdudi, the founder of the Indo-Pakistani Jama'at-i-Islami party, has inspired many fundamentalists Muslims worldwide. The term has become a pivotal one in the current fundamentalist vocabulary. The concept of "new *jahiliyya*", according to radical Islamic perceptions, targeted modernity and Western societies that have rejected the divinity of God and God's sovereignty, and hence have legitimized themselves through purely man-made criteria. This definition also epitomizes, in the radical fundamentalist view, the combination of godlessness, barbarism, decadence, and ignorance prevailing among these modern impious societies, conditions similar to those of pre-Islamic Arabia. Muslim societies experiencing the process of Westernization are warned by radical fundamentalists lest they be infected by the evils of the "new *jahiliyya*".[22] The concept of *jahiliyya* also seems to have taken hold, to some degree, among radical groups in Indonesia. New recruits to the Muslim militia, Laskar Mujahidin, were exposed to the concept of *jahiliyya* during their preparation for fighting against Christians in the Maluku Islands and in Poso in Central Sulawesi. These new recruits were repeatedly told in study groups that the situation in the Western world was comparable the "darkness" and *jahiliyya* that prevailed in Mecca before Islam emerged.[23] Many educated Muslims in Indonesia are familiar with this reactualized definition of *jahiliyya*, if only for the reason that the writings of both Sayyid Qutb and Abul-A'la al-Mawdudi have been translated into Indonesian and that their ideas have exerted a certain appeal in Indonesia.[24] Even Qutb's final book and his most popular one, *Ma'alim fi al-tariq* ("Signposts on the Road"), published in 1964, was translated into Indonesian.[25] This book defied Nasserism in Egypt, rejecting its secular, nationalist, and socialist–ideological basis. A formative and inspiring intellectual platform for a radical fundamentalist world-view, the book also provided the grounds for the laying of charges brought by the Egyptian court against members of the Muslim Brothers, including Sayyid Qutb himself, of conspiracy to over-throw the government and eventually led to the execution of Qutb and other leaders of the Brothers.[26] The theme of *jahiliyya* in the sense of the "modern Age of Ignorance" was central in Indonesia as early as the 1950s for activists of Persatuan Islam (PERSIS: "Muslim Union"), an association that arose in Indonesia in the 1920s representing a variation of the Islamic modernist stream of thought. This *jahiliyya* theme was articulated by Muhammad Isa Anshary, one of the leading spokesmen of Persis during the 1950s, in a book published in 1949. There are some conceptual parallels between Persis and two of its generational counterparts, Abul-A'la al-Mawdudi and Hasan al-Bana (1906–49), the founder of the Muslim Brothers. The rhetoric of fundamentalist Islam used by Persis is much the same as that employed by al-Mawdudi and al-Bana. The theme of "the modern Age of Ignorance" that threatens humankind with disaster and the necessity of Islamic law for a modern Muslim society, is shared by al-Mawdudi, al-Bana's followers, and the activists of Persis.[27]

The vigilance and animosity of radical Muslim fundamentalists toward the "infidels" is also revealed through the concept of *hijra*. Originally *hijra* meant the flight of the Prophet Muhammad and his followers from Mecca to Medina in AD 622, although it now indi-cates a historical epoch. Sayyid Qutb is again associated with the reactualization of the *hijra*. According to Qutb, devout Muslims, living in a society at a stage of *jahiliyya*, are required to carry out an act of *hijra* in order create their own community of true believers, before transforming that society into a genuinely Islamic one. *Hijra* therefore implies that "Islam and *jahiliyya* cannot coexist".[28] Some radical groups in the Middle East have used the term *hijra* to denote a temporary operational withdrawal in order to portray themselves as victors. Both concepts of *hijra* and *jahiliyya* also appear to have taken hold in the religious–political world-view of Osama bin Laden, the leader of al-Qa'ida.[29] In Indonesia, the concept of *hijra* has had a clear impression on the doctrine of the "Ngruki Network", the alleged historical antecedent of Jama'ah Islamiyah. Members of the network used the term *hijra* to denote their escape from Indonesia to Malaysia in 1985.[30] The name of the organization, Jama'ah Islamiyah, may also be linked, among other things, with the concept of *hijra*, in the sense of building an Islamic community of "true believers" as a necessary precondition for building the Islamic state.

Typically, the world-view of radical Muslim fundamentalists in Indonesia is filled with various images of enemies, the "infidels". In recent years, Indonesian Christians have come to be regarded by radical fundamentalists as a significant enemy. According to common radical fundamentalist perceptions, the Christians are dangerous enemies of Islam; they embody the crusaders, and are emissaries of a hostile religion. Christians trigger a hostile collective memory in the minds of radical Muslims, who are oriented toward the remote past. The Indonesian local context is also likely to feed the hostility of radical Muslims toward Christians, who constitute 8–9 percent of the Indonesian population. Years of missionary activity, and past antagonism showed by the Dutch colonial administration toward Islam, have made many Muslims in Indonesia suspicious and hostile toward the churches. Radical Muslims regard Christian proselytizing to be a threat to Islamic foundations.[31] Tensions between Muslims and Christians, including violent incidents which have been aggravated in recent years, can largely be explained by local circumstances that have little to do with radical fundamentalism. Nevertheless, the hostile rhetoric of radical Muslims has added fuel to the fire. This is clearly illustrated in the case of the Maluku Islands. Laskar Jihad tried hard to transform the local conflict on the islands, which started at the beginning of 1999, from a local dispute into an intensified inter-religious conflict between Islam and Christianity. The Islamic radical organization, Forum Komunikasi Ahlu Sunnah wal-Jama'ah (FKAWJ, "Communication Forum of the Followers of the Sunna"), which established Laskar Jihad, labeled those Christians in Maluku who allegedly attacked Muslims as *kafir harbi* – infidels who belonged to *dar al-harb* ("the territory of war"). According to the classical Islamic definition, *dar al-harb* is permanently in conflict with *dar al-Islam* ("the territory of Islam").[32] It is argued that in the case of the Laskar Jihad movement labeling the Christians in Maluku as such, they provided a religious license to kill them.[33] Another case that reveals the deep animosity among radical fundamentalists in Indonesia toward Christians was the bombings against Christian churches on Christmas Eve 2000 in ten Indonesian cities.

The ethnic-Chinese minority, constituting 3–4 percent of the Indonesian population, are also exposed to hostile attitudes by radical Muslims in Indonesia. Resentment of the Chinese has always been strong in Indonesia and dates back to the colonial period.[34] Always enjoying a significant role in the economy, the Chinese, the "others", have traditionally been the subject of envy, suspicion, hatred, and violence. The fact that many Chinese are also Christians, to a degree that the latter term is often used as a euphemism for the former,[35] makes them even more vulnerable. In many cases the attacks on churches also constitute a form of anti-Chinese violence. The widespread Muslim belief that the Chinese finance Christian missionary activity, also nourishes hostile emotions.[36] Radical Muslims in Indonesia have used potentially conflicting relations between Muslims and Chinese to their own interests. Radical Islamic groups were often involved in the growing religious and violent ethnic strife, which intensified shortly before Suharto's fall from power in 1998. Communists are also a target for Indonesian radical Muslims' animosity.[37] The atheist Communists are portrayed as enemies by radical Muslims elsewhere, who regard them as a bitter enemy and an avowed ideological rival. In the Indonesian context, this perception is also aggravated by the position reserved for Communism in the Indonesian collective memory as the historical enemy due to the failed coup attempt of September 30–October 1, 1965. The exact parameters of the involvement of

Partai Komunis Indonesia (PKI, Communist Party of Indonesia) in this affair are still unclear.[38]

In looking for enemies, radical Muslims in Indonesia do not limit themselves to the local context. They identify enemies across the globe. In this sense their "list of enemies" appears to be almost a replica of such images shared by radical fundamentalists in the Islamic world. Thus, for example, the West, in particular the United States, appears as an enemy through their prism. Anti-American sentiments in Indonesia have been increasingly galvanized recently by American military action in Afghanistan and Iraq. Radical Muslims are identifiable as those who attempt to feed hostile sentiments toward the United States. Even anti-Semitism or anti-Jewish sentiments have also taken hold among hardline Muslims in Indonesia, even though Indonesia is home to only a tiny number of Jews. Anti-Israel and anti-Zionist sentiments are also expressed.[39] In radical Muslim rhetoric, anti-Zionism, anti-Semitism, anti-Christianity, anti-Western sentiments, anti-Americanism, and even anti-Communism, are interchangeable terms to define the enemy, and are often expressed in the same breath.[40] The Laskar Jihad rhetoric is strongly inclined to join together Zionists (*Zionis*) and the Crusaders (*Salibis*), or the Zionists and the Christians/the West, as enemies and partners in a "conspiracy" against Islam.[41] Anti-Chinese feelings are added to this xenophobic rhetoric. A relatively intensive form of this rhetoric characterizes some radical Muslim groups, which are oriented toward political activity and involvement. Significant among them are Komiti Indonesia Solidaritas Dunia Islam (KISDI "Indonesian Committee for Islamic World Solidarity") and Dewan Dakwah Islamiyah Indonesia (DDII, "The Indonesian Islamic Preaching Council"), or for short, Dewan Dakwah, and its periodical *Media Dakwah*. Dewan Dakwah, in particular, is a vivid example of this kind of rhetoric.[42] Dewan Dakwah was established in 1967; its roots trace back to the Masyumi party. It has even been argued that the roots of many presentday Muslim radical groups in Indonesia can be traced back to the Masyumi,[43] which committed itself to establishing Indonesia as an Islamic state, and was banned in the early 1960s. Dewan Dakwah shows a strong commitment to the linkage between Islam and politics, and expresses through its publication *Media Dakwah* hardline and militant scripturalist Islamic perceptions. As such it is said to be located on the radical Islamic fringe.[44] Robert W. Hefner argues, however, that Dewan Dakwah is an umbrella association of reformist Muslims with varied political ideas, rather than a genuinely fundamentalist organization. He regards the ideas in *Media Dakwah* to be the outcome of strong connections Dewan Dakwah have maintained for years in the Middle East, in Saudi Arabia and Kuwait in particular, as well as in Pakistan. *Media Dakwah* therefore serves as a broker for Middle Eastern Muslims' ideas.[45]

Radical fundamentalists in Indonesia also find in the global arena subjects and causes to sympathize with. Primarily, sympathy is expressed toward Muslims involved in conflicts in various parts of the globe. This was demonstrated in the case of the Islamic resistance in Afghanistan against the Soviet occupation during the 1980s. Then, several hundred radical Muslims from Indonesia joined the Islamic resistance, taking part in a formative collective experience of global *jihad*. During the 1990s radical Muslims in Indonesia expressed support for Muslims in the Kashmir conflict and for Muslims in Bosnia-Herzegovina. Members of the radical groups in Indonesia were also involved in the activity of the militant Islamic groups in the southern part of the Philippines. Solidarity with the Palestinian cause is also pronounced. During the war in Iraq, Saddam Hussein enjoyed sympathy amongst radical Muslims in Indonesia. For example, Habib Rizieq Shihab, the leader of the Jakarta-based radical organization Front Pembela Islam (FPI, the "Islamic Defenders' Front"), called, during the anti-war demonstrations in Indonesia, for volunteers to go to fight a *jihad* in Iraq. Radical fundamentalists in Indonesia share with radical fundamentalists in the wider Islamic world their objects of sympathy as well as their objects of hate. There is evidence indicating a unified vision among radical fundamentalists in the Islamic world that crosses borders and gives rise to a global solidarity, which is marked by Islamic zeal.

Transmission of Ideas and Ideological Interaction

The narrative of radical fundamentalism in Indonesia is strongly grounded in a complex series of cross-regional and global networks that have disseminated the ideas of other parts of the Muslim world. In the former discussed case of the Islamic modernist movement in the Malay-Indonesian world, the Middle East proved to be the source of the transmission of ideas. Through a growing interaction between the Middle East and Indonesia, a complex mechanism of dissemination of Islamic knowledge and ideas has become established over time. This complex, discussed more fully below, is likely to be a vehicle for dissemination of radical fundamentalism, side by side with other Islamic ideas and streams of thought. Indonesian students and scholars who study in various Islamic centers in the Islamic world seem to be a significant conduit for transmitting radical fundamentalist ideas to Indonesia. Conspicuous among them are those who have studied in Saudi Arabia and Egypt. Both these countries have been for many years the preferred destination for Indonesians in search of Islamic knowledge. This partly explains, for example, the appeal that the Egyptian Muslim Brothers, regarded to be the forefathers of contemporary fundamentalism, have among Muslim Indonesians.[46] It can also partially explain the appeal that the puritan Wahhabi doctrine has had among Indonesians. In recent years, the Wahhabi world-view, originally from Arabia, has become closely associated with *salafi* conceptions, as both call for a return to the pure way of the pious ancestors. A similar terminological phenomenon can be found in Indonesia. Followers of the Wahhabi puritan interpretation of Islam prefer to describe it as "*Salafi Islam*". Ideas of this stream of Islamic thought have been disseminated into Indonesia both through the Saudi-financed Institute for Islamic and Arabic Studies (LIPIA) in Jakarta, and through the increasing number of Indonesians who have studied religion at Saudi universities.[47] Ja'far Umar Thalib, the head of Laskar Jihad, studied at LIPIA during the 1980s for three years, before later spending two years (1988–9) fighting the Soviets with the Afghan *mujahidin*. Initially, he joined one of the *mujahidin* factions affiliated with Saudi Arabia and subsequently he supported another faction, a strict *salafi* one, which was regarded to be a Saudi "principality". In 1991 he went to Yemen to widen his insights into Wahhabi teaching. He made efforts to propagate the Wahhabi–Salafi message in Indonesia after his return home in 1993. In 1994 he established a *pesantren* (Islamic school) in Yogyakarta, and a community, Jama'ah Ihya al-Sunnah (the "Association for Revitalizing the Sunna"). Conceptually, this community focused on strict Islamic pietism and puritanism, returning to the model of *al-salaf al-salih* and hoping to build an Islamic society, yet avoiding the political aspects of Islam, such as the idea of establishing an Islamic state. Much of the activity of this group included a *da'wa* and was directed to a large extent toward the Muslim students' discussion groups, known as *kelompok pengajian*, or *halaqa* ("study group"), which have spread since the 1980s throughout many "secular" campuses in Indonesia. In a similar vein to radical fundamentalist groups in the Middle East, such as Egypt, most of the students who joined Jama'ah Ihya al-Sunnah came from scientific and technical disciplines. In the beginning of 1998 this Wahhabi–Salafi movement started to change its orientation from non-political *da'wa* into political activism. This happened against a background of the increasing crisis on the eve of Suharto's political defeat. With the establishment of FKAWJ by Ja'far Umar Thalib, the members of Jama'ah Ihya al-Sunnah became the backbone of the new centralized organization. The shift of the orientation in Wahhabi–Salafi circles in Indonesia became further evident with the establishment of Laskar Jihad by Ja'far Umar Thalib in January 2000 as the paramilitary wing of FKAWJ. Many followers of the Wahhabi–Salafi discussion groups responded to the call from Laskar Jihad to join a *jihad* against the Christians on the Maluku Islands.[48]

Dewan Dakwah was also involved in diffusing Wahhabi–Salafi ideas to Indonesia. Since 1973 Dewan Dakwah has functioned as the representative in Indonesia of Rabitat al-'Alam al-Islami ("Muslim World League"), which is one of the major organizations used by Saudi Arabia to propagate Wahhabi–Salafi ideas. In the mid-1980s many Indonesian students studied in Saudi Arabia and Pakistan under the sponsorship of Dewan Dakawh. It was a project aimed at training Muslim believers for *da'wa* activities to oppose Christian missionaries.[49] Hundreds of Indonesians also travel each year to study *salafism* in religious schools in Yemen.[50] Some of these students return home with a radical Islamic world-view. It is likely that radical fundamentalist ideas have found their way to Indonesia, too, through Indonesian pilgrims returning from the *hajj*, bringing back with them Islamic ideas and streams of thought they have been exposed to during this massive gathering of Muslims from all over the world. Teachers of religion and Arabic, as well as preachers from the Middle East, may also function as a conduit for the transmission of extreme Islamist beliefs. It is true, furthermore, that radical fundamentalist ideas have arrived in the Indonesia archipelago from other Muslim areas apart from Egypt and Arabia. Pakistan is considered to play a role in this regard. Sojourns in Pakistan, as well as Arabia and Egypt, can be identified as milestones in the strengthening of belief of radical Indonesian Muslims. Many were also exposed to the ideology of "global *jihad*" during the 1980s in the formative radical experience of the resistance to the Soviet Union's occupation of Afghanistan as well as during training they received in Afghanistan and Pakistan.

Ideological texts have also played a considerable role in inspiring radical fundamentalist perceptions among Indonesians and in motivating local radical Muslims. Muslims in Indonesia have been widely exposed to formative texts in fundamentalist thinking. Because not many Indonesians can read Arabic fluently (even though many studied the language as part of their Islamic religious education), the access of Indonesian Muslims to formative fundamentalist texts has to be facilitated through translations into the native tongue, Bahasa Indonesia. Among them are the writings of Hasan al-Banna, the founder of the Muslim Brotherhood and a prominent ideological forefather of Islamic fundamentalism in the Islamic world. Al-Banna's writings are familiar to many educated Indonesian Muslims,[51] and he has also inspired Abu Bakar Ba'asyir, the alleged spiritual leader of Jama'ah Islamiyah.[52] The ideas of Sayyid Qutb, which have inspired radical fundamentalism in the entire Sunni Islamic world, are also well known among educated Muslims in Indonesia, and have left a clear imprint on radical Muslims in Indonesia; as have the ideas of Abul-A'la al-Mawdudi. The three – Qutb, al-Mawdudi, and al-Banna – are among the most prominent Muslim authors whose writings have been read and translated into Malay-Indonesian in recent decades.[53]

Even though Indonesia is home to a vast Muslim community that is dominantly Sunnite, radical Shi'ite revolutionary thought and writings have also found their way to the archipelago. Although Ayatollah Khomeini, the leader of the Iranian revolution, seems to have little appeal in Southeast Asia, the writings of Dr 'Ali Shari'ati (1933–77), considered to be a distinguished formative intellectual of the Iranian revolution, has won considerable popularity in both Indonesia and Malaysia, where his books have been translated, alongside translations of the writings of the key figures of radical Sunnite fundamentalism. Shari'ati's works first reached Indonesia through Indonesian students who read them in the United States. During the 1980s, many translations of Shari'ati's books and tracts subsequently appeared in Indonesia. The popularity of his writings and the impact his ideas have had among Muslims in Indonesia is explained largely by his egalitarian approach to Muslim society and his attacks on corrupt religious leadership. The exposure to the writings of Shari'ati and other Iranian thinkers in Indonesia has even aroused an interest in Shi'ism amongst the intellectual elite. And there are some elements in Indonesia who have not been deterred by the Shi'ite character of the Iranian revolution; rather, they have been inspired by its vivid model.[54]

Radical fundamentalists in the Islamic world have proved themselves to be quick and skilful in using modern communications technology to propagate their message, making increasing use of the internet. In this way, Muslims in Indonesia are exposed quickly and intensively to the information and ideas of radical fundamentalist organizations from the center of the Islamic world. The Internet even seems to strengthen a sense of participation in the "global *jihad*". Radical fundamentalists in Indonesia also host websites and distribute CDs and VCDs for propagation, as well as audio tapes and videos. There are also radical Muslim groups that have their own publications. Even radio broadcasts are run by some radical fundamentalists groups. Ja'far Umar Thalib, in particular, relied heavily on new communications technologies, propagating the *salafi* message and campaigning for the *jihad* in Maluku.[55] A significant role in propagating radical Islamic message is also played by certain private Islamic schools, run by clerics who preach Islamic radical perceptions.

Another conspicuous aspect in the current narrative of radical Islamic fundamentalism in Indonesia is the prominent role performed by Arabs, especially by those of Hadrami or Yemeni descent. Abu Bakar Ba'asyir is one of those with a Hadrami background, as was the late Abdullah Sungkar, who founded, with Ba'asyir, in the late 1970s, the "Ngruki Network". Similarly, Habib Rizieq Shihab, the leader of the Front Pembela Islam, was born to a family of Hadrami *sayyids*. Many top leaders of the latter organization are also in this community. Ja'far Umar Thalib, who headed Laskar Jihad until its disbandment in October 2002, is also a Hadrami Arab.[56] The fact that Osama bin Laden was born to a family which shares its heritage with these leaders of radical fundamentalist groups in Indonesia, and that Yemenis play a significant role in the global network of al-Qa'ida, perhaps make it tempting to point to the "Hadrami/Yemeni connection" of the "global *jihad*".

The Historical Perspective

The narrative of the introduction of Islam to Indonesia, as well as to other parts of Southeast Asia, is dotted with significant question marks. A paucity of data and conflicting evidence means that the earliest history of Islam in Southeast Asia is unclear and consequently there are multiple theories on fundamental unanswered questions.[57] India, partly through the Indian coastal settlements of Arab-Indian communities, carried out an important role as a preliminary conduit for diffusing Islamic belief and knowledge to the remote Indonesian archipelago. A dissemination of the Islamic message was performed mainly through the sea routes. But it was only in the eighteenth century that the Middle East began to take the lead in the spread of Islamic ideas and knowledge to Indonesia. That is, the prominence of the role played by the Middle East in shaping the nature of the "Islamic space" in Indonesia began to unfold about five centuries after the appearance of the earliest clear signs of local adoption of Islam in Indonesia, in the northern part of Sumatra. This pattern of dissemination of Islamic ideas and knowledge from the Middle East to Indonesia has marked both the old Islamic religious traditions and new ones, including the Sufi traditions, which are well established in Indonesia and played a leading role in the preliminary stages of the arrival of Islam to Indonesia.

The strengthening role of the Middle East in terms of the growth of Islam in the Indonesian archipelago can be viewed as part of an increasing interaction between the two regions. This increasing interaction resulted from a complex mix of technological, economic, and political factors. The accumulative affect of several developments which took place in the latter half of the nineteenth century in terms of communications between the Middle East and the Malay-Indonesian world was remarkable: the establishing of permanent maritime routes of steamships between Southeast Asia and the Red Sea; the opening of the Suez Canal in 1869;[58] the developments of journalism in both the Middle East and the Malay-Indonesian world. Of great importance was the increasing waves of immigration of the Hadramis to Southeast Asia, which began in the latter half of the eighteenth century and accelerated during the nineteenth century. This was due to the marked improvement of the transportation between Southeast Asia and the Middle East. The Hadramis, who were largely involved in trade between the two regions, have shown themselves as notable cultural brokers. It must be noted that the leading role played by Muslims traders from India in the propagation of Islam in the Malay-Indonesian archipelago for almost four centuries ended in the seventeenth century, when they were ousted by the Dutch East India Company (VOC), drawing to itself the trade of the Indonesian archipelago with India.[59] Another explanation for strengthening connections between Indonesia and the Middle East is that since Indonesia was ruled by the Dutch, a rival European power to Britain which ruled in South Asia, the commercial and cultural contacts between Asian Muslims of the two regions were prohibited. Consequently, Muslims in Southeast Asia were encouraged to strengthen contacts with Muslims in the Middle East.[60]

On the political level, the strengthening connections between Indonesia and the Middle East can also be partly attributed to a softening of Dutch colonial policy on Islam in Indonesia toward the end of the nineteenth century. It was due to the concepts of Snouck Hurgronje, the architect of the revised policy, that the formally restrictive policy toward Islam in the Dutch East Indies was replaced by a more sophisticated program of controlling and restricting the political aspects of Islam. The Dutch colonial authorities therefore eased restrictions upon the Pilgrimage at the turn of the twentieth century. These restrictions, which had been in force during the nineteenth century, aimed at making the *hajj* difficult by means of taxation, passport restrictions, forcing returned pilgrims to take examinations before allowing them to use the title *hajji* and other regulations.[61] However, the change of policy did not remove Dutch suspicions of the political manifestations of Islam in general, and pan-Islamism in particular, including fears of the Ottoman Empire's involvement in Indonesian affairs until its collapse after World War I.[62]

Dissemination of Islamic Ideas to Indonesia

One of the most visible aspects of increasing relations and an inter-action between Indonesia and the Middle East was the remarkable transmission and dissemination of Islamic knowledge and ideas from the Middle East. Although the movement and traffic of people between these two parts of the world had always played a significant role in the process of Islamization, it was only in the eighteenth century that a multidimensional broad-scale complex of cross-regional and global networks was further developed. It is not surprising that this traffic of ideas has occurred in parallel to a further inclining of Islam in Indonesia, as has happened in other parts of the Malay world, toward orthodoxy. Thus a sense of affili-ation to the center of the Islamic world wad strengthened among Indonesian Muslims.

This network of so-called "cultural brokers" includes pilgrims who returned from Arabia with various Islamic ideas; "pilgrims of learning"[63] from Indonesia (Islamic scholars and students who searched for Islamic knowledge studied at religious centers in the Middle East, in Mecca, Medina, and Cairo in particular); and Indonesian scholars and students who, at the turn of the twentieth century, learned in Singapore about Islam. Singapore was then a vital regional Islamic center and carried out an intermediary role in the conveying of Islamic knowledge and ideas from the Middle East to the Malay-Indonesian world. Also of considerable importance was the function played by the Arab community, dominantly Hadramis, as cultural brokers between the two regions. Preachers and religious teachers from the Middle East also contributed directly to the process. Publications, and in particular printed journals, which began to make their mark toward the end of the nineteenth century in both the Middle East and Southeast Asia, also played a role in the increasing conceptual and intellectual interaction between the Middle East and Indonesia.

The *Hajj*: The annual gathering of Muslims from all over the world in Mecca for the fulfillment of the religious commandment of the *hajj*, the Pilgrimage, has exerted a tremendous religious effect for centuries, as a stirring collective experience, and as a demonstration of solidarity and integration of the manifold members of the *umma*. Many pilgrims have functioned in their homeland, after returning from the cosmopolitan encounter in Mecca, as cultural brokers and emissaries of the process of Islamic globalization. The Indonesian case reveals various aspects of this phenomenon. The Dutch colonial policy toward a possible political dimension of Islam in Indonesia was influenced to a large extent by a strong suspicion toward the *hajj*. The Dutch deeply mistrusted those who returned from the pilgrimage in Mecca, the *hajji*, viewing them as chief troublemakers and political propagandists. This suspicious attitude of the Dutch colonial government developed into a "hajiphobia" (*hajji-phobia*), a tendency to see every Muslim scholar as an enemy.[64] Political manifestations of Islam, including pan-Islamic ideas and sentiments, were viewed as a threat. In actual fact, the Indonesia Muslims in Mecca were exposed during the *hajj* to many different current ideas and streams of thoughts. The prestigious status they enjoyed as *hajji* facilitated their function as propagators of Islamic belief and ideas. Indonesian pilgrims, for example, were exposed to Wahhabi puritanism and militancy as early as the second half of the eighteenth century, very close to the time of the initial emergence of these ideas, and proceeded to disseminate them in their homeland.[65] In West Sumatra, Wahhabi ideas, brought across from Arabia, even developed at the beginning of the nineteenth century into a remarkable militant movement. Indeed, Indonesian Muslims were also exposed to varied pan-Islamic sentiments and anti-European and anti-colonial attitudes. The *hajj* also strengthened the *santri* element, the orthodox Muslims, in rural religious life in Indonesia, and played an important role in social change. Travel to Mecca and the Pilgrimage itself exposed people from villages to the outside world

and helped linked urban and rural Islam in Indonesia.[66] The returning pilgrims also functioned as dispensers of news. Reports brought
by the *hajji* about the Muslim world "were spread by word of mouth
from one person to another during conversations held in the village
restaurants or in the *langgar* [small prayer house] and the mosques,
especially after the evening prayers".[67] The number of Indonesians
who made the Pilgrimage to Mecca increased from the late nineteenth century onward. This was the result of the aforementioned
liberalization of the Dutch policy toward the *hajj,* the establishing of
steamship lines between the two regions, the opening of the Suez
Canal, and the increasing economic opportunities available to
Indonesians, which meant more of them could afford to make the
trip. Thus, for example, at the beginning of the 1910s the Indonesians
comprised almost 30 percent of all overseas pilgrims in Mecca.[68]

"Pilgrims of learning": Other major protagonists in the age-old
interaction between Indonesia and the Middle East are the "pilgrims
of learning", the Indonesian Islamic scholars and students who have
headed westward, for centuries, to Islamic centers in the Middle
East. They have played an important role in the process of
Islamization and the transmitting of Islamic ideas to Indonesia.
Many of them established themselves, after spending long periods
of study in the Middle East, as leaders of their own communities.
Their preferable destinations in the Middle East were mainly the two
Holy Cities in Arabia, mainly Mecca, to whose direction Muslims
all over the world turn daily in their prayer, and Medina. The religious importance of both cities as cosmopolitan Islamic centers is
strengthened by the annual *hajj.*[69] It has been argued that the fact
that the *Shafi'i* Islamic school of jurisprudence that predominates
both in Southeast Asia and the Hijaz, Hadramaut, and Egypt, seems
to have facilitated the movement of Indonesian scholars to Islamic
networks in the Middle East.[70]

Once in the Middle East, the cradle of Islam and a place of religious vitality, the Islamic scholars and students established
networks of *'ulama* and texts, while also playing a significant role in
translating religious books from Arabic into their own languages.
Thus they constituted an important vehicle in the dissemination of
Islam's beliefs, ideas, and knowledge from the Middle East to the

Malay-Indonesian world. In Mecca, as early as the sixteenth century, scholars from the Malay-Indonesian world started forming their own distinct community, known collectively as the *Jawa* (from *bilad al-Jawa*, the "lands of the Jawa", while the term *jawa* has been used by Arabic speakers as a synecdoche for Southeast Asia).[71] Numbers of this community studied for many years in Mecca and some even spent the rest of their lives there. In Mecca they could mingle with leading *'ulama* from different parts of the Muslim world, who brought with them varied Islamic traditions of learning. It also enabled them to become involved in the intellectual–religious attempts to reconcile the Great Tradition of Islam with its Little Tradition, or between "high religion", the Islamic orthodox tradition, which has a legal nature, and Sufi mystical traditions. Consequently, neo-Sufism, which came out of this attempt, impressed itself on Sufi *tariqat* in Indonesia. Indonesian scholars in Mecca also produced religious texts, books, and pamphlets in Malay with Arabic characters, known as *kitab jawi*. Many of them established their own circles of followers in their own mosques after their return to the archipelago, and even asserted modes of Islam, enjoying their prestigious status as those who had studied for years in the leading Islamic centers in Arabia. Another phenomenon attests to the close religious bonds between Muslims in Indonesia and Arabia: that is, for centuries, Indonesian Muslims turned to *'ulama* in Mecca and Medina for guidance in religious matters, requesting legal opinion (*fatwa*). This phenomenon is also connected to the *Jawa* colony or community in Mecca, since responsa to the requests for religious advice sent by Indonesian Muslims were also given by religious figures who belonged to this colony.[72]

Cairo has also been, for centuries, a preferred destination for Muslim scholars and students from the Middle East. The prestige of al-Azhar as an Islamic university, on the one hand, and the absence in Southeast Asia of long-established centres of Islamic learning enjoying a similar status, on the other, have ensured that Malay-Indonesian students have continued down the centuries to head for al-Azhar.[73] Many Indonesian graduates of al-Azhar have played significant positions in contemporary Indonesia in various fields, among them Islamic affairs, academic life, political activity, and journalism.

The community of the Malay-Indonesian students in Cairo showed a considerable vitality during the 1920s and the 1930s. Most of the community's members studied at al-Azhar; it was highly dynamic, and proved itself to be an effective channel for the dissemination of ideas of Islamic modernism from Egypt to Indonesia. In early twentieth-century Cairo, with its atmosphere of political and ideological ferment, the Malay-Indonesian students became acquainted with a rich variety of political debates and activity. They were largely exposed to pan-Islamic sentiments, including the "hot" issue of the abolition of the Caliphate (1924) and the political activity that followed it. The Caliphate question stirred, for a while, an interest in Indonesia as well.[74] These students were also exposed to anti-colonial attitudes and to the Islamic assertive concepts of the Muslim Brothers, as well as to the ideas of liberalism and secular nationalism. It is not surprising, then, that these students were a source of concern for the Dutch colonial authorities in Indonesia: in Cairo they were able to freely express their political sentiments, including their anti-colonial feelings. The unique opportunities that Cairo offered to Malay-Indonesian students in the 1920s are neatly summarized by a former student: "In Mecca one could study religion only; in Cairo, politics as well".[75]

In recent years young Indonesians have started to find al-Azhar less attractive, mainly due to its alleged intellectual decline, obsolete methods of teaching and learning, bureaucratic difficulties, and the poor living conditions.[76] In addition, universities in Europe and the US have become more desirable to young Indonesians wanting training in the sciences. Thus, a growing number of them are being sent to study in the United States and Europe, including those wishing to take advanced Islamic studies. Furthermore, Western-trained Indonesian scholars are alleged to have a better chance of success in their careers, and their impact at home increases, too.[77] Nevertheless, al-Azhar remains one of the most important centers of religious learning in the Islamic world and is still regarded as a prestigious destination for Indonesians who seek religious knowledge.[78]

The Hadramis – Cross-Cultural Brokers: Since the nineteenth century the Arab communities in Indonesia have shown themselves to be an energetic and influential element in Malay-Indonesian life.

Among them the Hadramis are remarkably dominant in number and vitality. In fact, individual Hadramis have played a significant role in the proselytization of the Malay-Indonesian world from the fifteenth century onward.[79] They were deeply involved in trade between the Middle East and Southeast Asia, which played an important role in the process of Islamization of the Malay-Indonesian world. Significant waves of immigration of the Hadramis to Southeast Asia only commenced in the second half of the eighteenth century, and accelerated during the nineteenth century. The increasing immigration of the Hadramis to the Indonesian archipelago resulted largely from the establishment of a steam-shipping route between Arabia and Indonesia, and the opening of the Suez Canal in 1869.[80] Since the latter half of the nineteenth century, the Arab presence in Southeast Asia contributed to the "refinement and the deepening of the Islamic ideas and practices which had remained largely superficial",[81] whereas in the preliminary stages they had introduced Islam to this part of the world as an outcome of their activities in trade.[82]

Economic imperatives lie behind Arab immigration to Indonesia. It was for this same reason that the flow of immigration from the Hadramaut started to quicken during the eighteenth century. These later waves of migration involved a highly significant movement of people. The earliest figures indicate that the Hadrami population in the Dutch East Indies in 1859 numbered 7,768 Arab men, women, and children. The official Dutch census of 1930 numbered 71,335 Arabs. It was estimated that by the mid-1930s around 110,000 people from Hadramaut lived abroad, nearly a third of the population, and the majority of the emigrant Hadramis lived in Indonesia, known then as the Dutch East Indies.[83]

Many of the Hadrami immigrants came from towns in Hadramaut and were involved in small-scale trade. Well trained in the art of commerce, they quickly assumed considerable economic power in trade, mainly as middle-men in economic transactions and as merchants of cross-cultural trade. This economic power was translated, remarkably, into a significant religious status as well. The native population looked upon Arabs as models of piety and the orthodox way of life, as people who were blessed with religious merit. Such attitudes among the native population were shown in particular toward the *sayyids,* who claimed descent from the Prophet Muhammad and belonged to the upper class. They were regarded to be the elite of the Islamic community in the Malay-Indonesian world. Even many non-*sayyid* Hadrami immigrants, who had lesser claim to expertise in Islam, were automatically accorded recognition in Islamic belief and knowledge by the locals. This was due largely to the fact that the Hadramis in Indonesia were mainly devout adherents of the faith and were more careful than the general Indonesian Muslims in their everyday religious observance. The prestigious position of the Hadramis among Indonesian Muslims also seems to have been fed by a long-standing opinion, which the Arab community in Indonesia did not attempt to dispel, which held that Arabs, as the original believers in Islam, should have a superior status to that of later Muslims. The Arabs, or the Hadramis, also enjoyed the benefit of not being seen as a foreign element by the locals, since their communities were ethnically mixed. Many members of these communities were married to indigenous Indonesian women or were born to Indonesian women, since there had been a strict embargo on female immigration from the Hadramaut.

It is not surprising, then, that many of the Arab immigrants in Indonesia became religious teachers and leaders. Their dominant religious position, social status, and their Middle Eastern origins, naturally positioned them at the forefront of the religious interaction between the Middle East and Indonesia. The role of the Hadramis as cultural brokers between the two regions was also encouraged by the strong links and affiliations they maintained with the Middle East, due to their considerable involvement in cross-regional commerce. They also quite often sent their children back to their countries of origin to receive an education and retained a great deal of interest in the events and developments in Arab countries. They subscribed to various journals and publications published in the Middle East. Noticeable also is the great importance that was given to the knowledge of Arabic. It is likely that the importance placed on command of the Arabic language also helped them to preserve their historical position as cultural brokers between the two regions.[84]

Through their economic achievements, religious prestige, and vitality, as well as their efforts to adapt themselves to modern contemporary needs, the Hadramis achieved a considerable influence not only in religious affairs, but also made a significant impact on economic, political, and social developments in Indonesia. The case of Islamic modernism in Indonesia and the strong effect it had on the local Hadrami community clearly demonstrate the important role of the Hadramis in the dissemination of ideas from the Middle East to Southeast Asia. The Hadrami community was a platform for the emergence of clear and loud calls for religious revival, led mainly by Jam'iyyah al-Islah wal-Irshad al-'Arabiyyah ("Arab Association for Reform and Guidance"), which generated a substantial change in religious thinking. Furthermore, the revivalist approach that emerged in this community was largely implemented in the field of education and in other aspects of life of the community. Inspired by progressive and egalitarian ideas, the Hadrami awakening brought about various changes through a conflict with the traditional centers of power. During the 1920s and the 1930s this "trade diaspora" and community of cultural brokers even exported its vitality and spirit of reform back to the Hadramaut. A growing number of Hadrami reformers who returned during the 1930s to settle in the Hadramaut supported this process. Although the spirit of reform faced mounting opposition and the outcome fell far short of the aspirations of the Hadramis in the Dutch East Indies, this transmission of ideas back to the Hadramaut is a rare case, in the narrative of the interaction between the Middle East and the entire Malay-Indonesian world, of the reverse flow of ideas; the narrative is one dominated by a one-way transmission of concepts, from the Middle East to the Malay-Indonesian world.[85]

The vitality of the Hadrami community in Indonesia, and in particular its deep involvement in religious matters, fed the Dutch colonial authorities' distrust of the Arabs in the archipelago. The Dutch increasingly suspected them to be fanatic propagandists of Islam and supporters of pan-Islamism. They feared that the Arabs in Indonesia would use the rise of pan-Islamic sentiments in Indonesia to undermine their colonial authority; they were also concerned about the sympathy that many Hadramis had clearly shown to their rivals, the Ottoman Empire.[86] This attitude largely influenced the Dutch decision to exclude the Hadramis from the liberal immigration policy they followed at the beginning of the twentieth century. It is interesting that, in making this decision, the Dutch were largely following advice of their influential adviser to Islamic affairs, Snouck Hurgronje, who supported the revoking of restrictions on travel and residence, and even removed restrictions on the *hajj*.[87]

Publications: Various kinds of publications also contributed in the modern era to the diffusion of Islamic ideas and knowledge to Indonesia. Religious tracts and texts, and other religious publications, arrived in Indonesia through the growing movement of people.[88] Important among them was the category of the *kitab jawi,* published in Mecca by the *Jawa* colony. The Hadramis in Indonesia, who played a significant role in the field of journalism, also contributed to the process of the dissemination of ideas and knowledge, using the platform of their publications. Arab printers existed in Indonesia as early as the 1850s. The greatest expansion of the field of print took place in the 1910s and 1920s with a growth of variety of periodicals, in Arabic, Malay, and mixed languages.[89] Efforts made by the Hadrami community in the field of printing, particularly newspapers, alongside its considerable efforts to establish modern educational institutions, are regarded to be a crucial part of the process of the Hadrami "awakening" in Indonesia in the first four decades of the twentieth century. This process was strongly connected with the emergence of Islamic modernism in Indonesia. The growth of a new vision of education, motivated by Islamic modernist perceptions and defying traditional and obsolete educational systems, is regarded to have had a significant importance in the Hadrami "awakening". As part of the new outlook on education and teaching, Hadrami students were encouraged to read the original newspapers published by their community and to contribute to them. Reading rooms were opened up.[90] The Hadrami or Arab-Muslim publications showed an interest in the wider Islamic world, particularly in centers such as Cairo, Istanbul, and Mecca. Similarly, they were used as a platform for Islamic issues and for articulating the idea of pan-Islamism. They included expressions of sympathy as well as concern toward the Ottoman Empire,[91] which at that time was in a prolonged state of decline and was close to its formal end, which came with the abolition of the Caliphate in 1924.

The instrumental role played by the print media in the transmission of ideas from the Middle East to Indonesia was clearly demonstrated in the case of Islamic modernism. It has had a particular impact on the "Islamic space" in Indonesia. Rashid Rida's *al-Manar* contributed to relaying 'Abduh's Islamic modernist ideas from Egypt to the Malay-Indonesian world. *Al-Manar*, published in Cairo, was circulated in the Malay-Indonesian world, even conducting a quasi-dialogue with local Islamic modernists. Its impact on the Malay-Indonesian world may be seen in one of the names that was given to the modernist group in the Malay-Indonesian world – "*Kaum al-Manar*" ("The *Manar* Group"). Even though the Dutch colonial government attempted to prevent its entry into the Indonesian archipelago, *al-Manar* was successfully circulated in a number of underhand ways. It was smuggled into the archipelago; brought by *hajjis* upon their return from Arabia, where the journal was readily available; and brought by students returning from Cairo, Mecca, and Medina. This journal contributed to the spread of modernist ideas by creating the impetus to publish similar journals in the Malay-Indonesian world. Notable among them were the previously mentioned Singapore-based *al-Imam* (1906–8) and *al-Munir* (1911–16). *Al-Imam* came to be regarded as one of the most important intellectual vehicles of the modernist Islamic voice in the Malay-Indonesian world. Although it was based in Singapore, a high proportion of *al-Imam* correspondence came from Indonesia, particularly Sumatra. A few years after *al-Imam* ceased to be published, *al-Munir* was founded in Padang (West Sumatra) by leaders of the *Kaum Muda*.[92] *Seruan Azhar* and *Pilehan Timur*, journals which were published during the 1920s by the Malay-Indonesian students in Cairo, also made their contribution to the transmission of Islamic modernist ideas to Indonesia.

Arabic journals from the Middle East were involved to a significant degree in the discussed process of dissemination of ideas. Various newspapers imported from the Middle East to Indonesia, from the late nineteenth century onward, also indicated a desire among literate Muslims to learn about events taking place in the outside world, in particular in the Islamic world. Even copies of the

famous periodical *al-'Urwa al-Wuthqa* ("The Indissoluble Bond"),
published in Paris in 1884 by the two forefathers of Islamic modernism, Jamal al-Din al-Afghani and Muhammad 'Abduh, found
their way to Indonesia. The growing interest of Indonesian Muslims
in the Islamic world, and in particular in the Middle East, can be
largely attributed to the spreading of pan-Islamic ideas among them.
Naturally, conspicuous among the readers of Middle Eastern newspapers were the Arab Hadramis. At the beginning of the twentieth
century, many of them maintained close contacts with their places
of origin in Arabia and followed events in the Middle East, sub-
scribing to various newspapers published there.[93] Malay journals
published in Singapore, the site of vivid Islamic activity in the late
nineteenth early twentieth centuries, were also a vehicle for disseminating ideas in Islamic context. Malay journals in Singapore of that
time largely used Middle Eastern presses, in particular the Egyptian
press, as a source of news, and as the inspiration for a journalistic
style.[94] The influence of the Egyptian press is also evident in Arabic
newspapers published in Singapore during the 1930s.[95] It must be
noted that the Middle Eastern media of that time showed some
degree of interest in Malay-Indonesian Muslims. Thus, newspapers
in Egypt, Constantinople (Istanbul), and Beirut had correspondents
in Indonesia and in Singapore as early as the late nineteenth century
who regularly reported on the mistreatment of their fellow Muslims
by the Dutch.[96]

Singapore at the Beginning of the Twentieth Century: The Straits
Settlements, and Singapore in particular, proved to be an intellectual nerve-center of the Islamic renaissance at the beginning of the
twentieth century. This is clear from the significant role they carried
out in the process of disseminating the reformist message of Islamic
modernism to the Malay-Indonesian world. In 1901 the total population of Singapore was about 228,500 people. The majority of them,
72 percent of the population, were Chinese. Most of the others came
from the Malay peninsula and from the Indonesian archipelago. The
Arab community, which was close-knit and linked by its Hadrami
past and present, and its religious language, numbered around just
1,000. This vital community, however, soon took a position of leadership within the larger community of the Malay Muslims. The *Jawi*

Peranakan, mainly local-born offspring of unions between South Indian Muslim traders and Malay women, also constituted a significant intellectual element in the Malay-Muslim community in Singapore. They numbered approximately 600 in 1901. The *Jawi Peranakan* ranked next to the Arabs within the Malay-Muslim community in Singapore, and enjoyed a reputation for intelligence and language ability and contributed, to a very significant degree, to the flourishing of Malay journalism in Singapore from the 1870s to the beginning of the twentieth century.[97]

There are several explanations as to what made Singapore such a vivid and creative center of Islamic life, learning, and publications. Its location on the sea routes of Southeast Asia made Singapore an important focal point for the movement of people and goods as well as a dynamic metropolis. To this obvious advantage, other explanations, such as the Islamic context per se, can be added. Direct British colonial control of Singapore enabled all the people, including Muslims, to attain a degree of intellectual freedom that was not permitted under the Dutch colonial regime of the Indies or the Sultans in Malaya. As such, Singapore was a base for many foreign Muslim scholars. Muslim students from the region who could not afford go to the Middle East for their Islamic studies found in Singapore a viable alternative, where they studied at the feet of Islamic scholars from the Hadramaut and Indonesia, many of whom had themselves studied in Mecca. Singapore was also a major port for Muslim pilgrims, many of them from Indonesia, to avoid the restrictive regulations on the *hajj* imposed by the Dutch colonial authorities, which were only removed in 1902. A number of those Indonesians stayed several years in Singapore prior to their travel to Arabia, in order to earn money for the passage.[98]

Religious Teachers and Preachers from the Middle East: Preachers and teachers, mainly in the fields of religious studies and Arabic from the Middle East, were also involved in the cross-regional dissemination of Islamic ideas linking Indonesian Muslims to the hub of the Muslim world. Teachers from Mecca, Egypt, and Istanbul are reported to have arrived in Southeast Asia as early as the sixteenth century. Bringing with them news about the continuing advance of the Ottoman Turks, they generated sympathy for the

Ottoman Empire.[99] Due to the growing interaction between the two regions, the presence of teachers from the Middle East in Indonesia also increased. In recent decades, largely out of political–ideological interests, Arab countries have been involved in efforts to send missionaries, preachers, and teachers to Indonesia. Notable efforts along these lines have been made by both Saudi Arabia and Egypt: scholarships are offered annually by the Saudis and by al-Azhar University to Indonesian students. Mona Abaza notes that the "bargaining over the legitimacy of Islamic discourse" since the colonial era was divided between Egypt and Saudi Arabia.[100] The efforts made by both countries in Indonesia, home to such a vast Muslim community, seems to be another manifestation of this bargaining.

The War Cry of Jihad in Indonesia

The war cry of *jihad* and the use of force have largely marked the historical breakthrough of the spread of Islam. Whereas Persia and India were in the main Islamized through Muslim military and political force, the Malay-Indonesian archipelago did not undergo such a process. Muslim armies did not occupy its land in order to carry the message of Islam. There were isolated cases of the use of force by certain Malay-Indonesian Muslims rulers to convert their people. M. C. Ricklefs says that an Indonesian Islamic state, upon being founded, sometimes resorted to warfare to spread the message of Islam. He adds that sixteenth-century Sumatra and Java and seventeenth-century Sulawesi provide examples of this, explaining that though these wars were not primarily in order to spread Islam, the fact remains that Islamization often followed upon conquest and that Islam in Indonesia was spread "not only by persuasion and commercial pressures, but by the sword as well".[101] Anyhow it is not uncommon to argue that the process of Islamization in the region has been carried out, to a large extent, in a peaceful way.[102] A. H. Johns clearly summarizes this approach: "The spread of Islam in Southeast Asia was hesitant, modest and discreet; what was achieved in one century in the Middle East took virtually a millennium in Southeast Asia."[103] Therefore, there is a great deal of contemporary interest in the war cry of *jihad* which has been sounded in Indonesia in the modern era.

The early nineteenth century witnessed a significant case of Islamic revivalism in the Indonesian archipelago known as the Wahhabi-inspired Padri movement in Minangkabau (in West Sumatra). Islam in Minangkabau during the late eighteenth century still exhibited a highly syncretic form. In spite of a gradually increasing influence of Islam, which started its expansion there in the early sixteenth century, a large proportion of the population remained attached to their animistic beliefs. Similarly, *adat* as both local customary law and as an inner world-view of Minangkabau was profoundly significant. But Minangkabau of the late eighteenth century faced a variety of political, social and cultural tensions; fresh currents from the Islamic world outside which had been brought back to the villages in Minanagkabau, mainly by the returning *hajis*, challenged the traditional order. The existing methods of the traditional society were found inadequate for settling disputes in the face of increasing commerce and trade, and widespread threatening banditry. That was the moment for the advocates of Islam from within, emerging from Islamic revivalist movements, to attempt to elevate Islamic law to a position of pre-eminence. Around 1803 there swept into this setting a religious fermented, puritan and militant current of thought from the heartlands of Islam. It would later develop into a highly energetic puritanical movement known as the Padri movement, which was created by three *hajjis*. The three, known as Padris after the port of Pedir in Aceh from which most of the Minangkabau pilgrims sailed to Arabia, were deeply influenced by the initial success of the Wahhabi movement in Arabia at that time. The three, who had returned from Mecca earlier that year, had witnessed the stirring episode of conquest of the holy city by an army of desert warriors. At the same time, warriors of a revivalist movement arose in Nejd (in Eastern Arabia) led by Muhammad Ibn 'Abd al-Wahhab (1703–92). Under the influence of the call of the Wahhabis to bring back the *shari'a* and for a return to the most fundamental tenets of the Prophet Muhammad and his Companions, the three *hajjis* were determined to launch a full-scale revival movement when they returned home. Following in the spirit of the Wahhabis, the Padri movement, engaged in *jihad* against the traditional *adat* order in Minangkabau. This order was regulated by local customs, either animist or Hindu-Buddhist, and as such was denounced by the movement as *jahili*. Taking control of a vast area, the movement imposed the *shari'a* and Islamic codes of behavior. Only at the end of the 1830s, after long years of war and Dutch military intervention, was the movement finally defeated. Despite its defeat, the Padri movement's revivalism is regarded in retrospect as a significant landmark in the history of Islamic renewal and reform in Indonesia. Its impact exceeded the geographical limits of Minangkabau in various ways. A strong defiance was embodied in the Padri revivalism of the Little Tradition of the *adat* through an attempt to raise the Great Tradition of orthodoxy to a position of the highest importance. The movement's revivalism eventually caused an increasing penetration of Islam into the fabric of Minangkabau society. It also brought about long-term gradual gains for the orthodoxy at the expense of the *tariqat*s, and enabled Wahhabi-inspired concepts to leave their mark in many parts of Indonesia.[104]

A series of peasants' revolts in Java in the nineteenth century were also marked by Islamic religious revivalism, millenarianism, extremism and militancy, even though they are considered primarily to be social and political movements. They were also marked by pan-Islamism and anti-Western characteristics. Many Muslims in the Middle East and North Africa in the second half of the nineteenth century, under the deep psychological impact of the conquests of Western imperialism, developed a growing peril of falling under Western domination. Hatred toward the *kafir* ("infidel") conquerors also developed among Indonesian Muslims. In this local case the anti-Western feelings developed into an expression of hatred toward the Dutch as the "enemies" of Islam. This process demonstrated the wide communication system established in the Islamic world by the pilgrims. Through it, news concerning any Muslim community could reach the most remote places of the Islamic world. This influence of the center of the Islamic world on Indonesian Muslims even expressed itself in cases of Islamic revivalism in Java, manifested through an inflaming millennial idea about the messianic figure of the *Mahdi*. It burst out in the peasants' revolt of Banten (in the northwest of Java) in the 1880s, and may have been influenced by the millennial movement of Mahadism in Sudan in the same decade. These manifestations of Islamic revivalism also included a vivid awareness among Indonesian Muslims that their country was regarded, in Islamic terms, as *dar al-Islam* ("the territory of Islam"), temporarily administrated by foreign rulers. Consequently, the call of waging *jihad* against the "infidel" rulers was also sounded.[105]

The war cry of *jihad* also had an effect on the Acehnese war against the Dutch, whose hold in Sumatra during the 1850s and 1860s was creeping up the north coast of the island. The Acehnese war began officially in 1873. In 1881 the local *'ulama* declared the war as *jihad*, or *perang sabil* (from *perang fi sabilillah*: "war in the cause/path of God"). A new lease of life was breathed into the Acehnese resistance, which became characterized by a religiously-inspired guerilla war led by the village *'ulama*. A growing interest among Indonesian Muslims in establishing connections with the hub of the Muslim world was also evident from this case. The Acehnese brought political pan-Islamic ideas into their conflict with the European colonial power and even attempted to win the support of the Ottoman Empire, with whom they had connections dating back to the sixteenth century. The Acehnese war ended in 1903. Only then did the Sultan of Aceh finally surrender to the Dutch, and the last obstacle to their full control of Sumatra was removed. Yet, on a symbolic level, for Islamists, the Acehnese resistance is regarded as a significant struggle against *kafir* colonial rule. Also, the concept of *perang sabil* imprinted itself in the local Acehnese context. So, in October 1945 the leading *'ulama* of Aceh marked the Indonesian War of Independence by placing it in an Islamic context, proclaiming the struggle against the Dutch as a Holy War, or *perang sabil*.[106]

About a century after the Padri movement, another Islamic militant cry was heard in West Java; calls for the establishment of an Islamic state in Indonesia were loudly echoed there. This happened in 1948 when the Darul Islam movement started, a *jihad* against Dutch colonialism. The movement was led by Sekarmadji Maridjan Kartosuwirjo (1905–62). Kartosuwirjo had, for several years, already been involved with Islamic military activity, including Hizbu'llah. Both Hizbu'llah and Sabili'llah, established during the Japanese Occupation (1942–5) and with Japanese consent, were the armed branches of the then major Islamic party, Masyumi. Early in 1948, the Darul Islam movement declared the setting up of

the Tentara Islam Indonesia ("Indonesian Islamic Army").
Inspired by classical Islamic perceptions, the movement also
termed its own territory *darul Islam* ("the territory of Islam") while
the territory that was held by the Dutch it termed *darul harb* ("the
territory of war"). From the end of 1948 onward the Darul Islam
movement made the Indonesian Republic, not the Dutch, its principal target, arguing that the secular Republican leaders of
Indonesia had made themselves as evil as the Dutch by rejecting
Islam as the sole foundation of Indonesia, and that they showed
hesitancy in the struggle of the young Indonesian Republic for
complete independence. In August 1949, Kartosuwirjo proclaimed
the establishment of the Negara Islam Indonesia ("The Islamic
State of Indonesia"). Referring to the metaphor of the Prophet
Muhammad's *hijra* ("emigration") from Mecca to al-Medina,
Kartosuwirjo renamed Cisampang, the village where the procla-
mation was made, Medina. Kartosuwirjo, who attributed much
ideological significance to the concept of the *hijra*, explained his
symbolic act in terms of being driven away from his headquarters
at Mount Sawal, his own Mecca, by the Republican troops.
According to the constitution of the newly proclaimed Islamic
state, the state guaranteed the implementation of Islamic law
within the Muslim community and granted the followers of other
religions freedom of worship. The head of the state, Kartosuwirjo,
was given the title of *Imam*. The *Imam* was to preside over a
Cabinet (Dewan Imamah). According to the constitution there
were to be three other bodies: Majlis Syuro (Arabic: *Majlis Shura*),
the "Parliament"; Dewan Syuro, the "Executive" of Majlis Syuro;
and Dewan Fatwa, chaired by grand *Mufti*, to advise the *Imam* and
his government.[107]

The war cry of Darul Islam in West Java spread to parts of Central
Java, to South Sulawesi, to South Kalimantan (Borneo), and to
Aceh, to include rebellious movements in these areas. The Darul
Islam rebellions were carried out under the banner of Islam, though
they exhibited other important aspects in addition to this dominant
religious color. Such tenacious and widespread rebellions greatly
worried the central government in Jakarta during the 1950s.[108] It was
not until the early 1960s that the Indonesian Army at last suppressed
the various rebellions. Kartosuwirjo himself was captured and

executed in 1962. It is of interest that Kartosuwirjo is considered to be a primary political inspiration for the militant "Ngruki Network", which emerged in Central Java in the 1970s and proved itself to be a significant hotbed and breeding ground for current Islamic radicalism in Indonesia. The commitment of this militant group and its offspring, Jama'ah Islamiyah, to fight for setting up an Islamic state in Indonesia, was largely influenced by the Kartosuwirjo model and Darul Islam rebellions and heavily depends on the latter experience. Veteran members of Darul Islam movements also joined the ranks of Jama'ah Islamiyah. Furthermore, it has been argued that the support network of Darul Islam in West Java was never entirely destroyed and that the underground networks of this movement appear to have persisted until the present day and have played a considerable role in the current narrative of Islamic radicalism in Indonesia.[109] The Darul Islam rebellion of South Sulawesi, in particular the image of its commander, Kahar Muzakkar (1921–65), also inspires militant Muslims today active in South Sulawesi. His son, Abdul Aziz Kahar Muzakkar, heads the Makassar-based radical Islamic organization Komite Pengerakan Syariat Islam (KPSI, "Committee to Uphold Islamic Law").

Summary and Reflections

Fundamentalism, writes Bruce B. Lawrence, "has historical antecedents, but no ideological precursors".[110] Indeed, the broader historical perspective of Indonesia does not seem to point to any ideological precursors for the current radical fundamentalism there. But a closer look at Indonesia's colonial history reveals various insights into Indonesian–Middle Eastern Islamic relations which highlight to some extent the background to the current globalized dimension of radical Islamic fundamentalism in Indonesia. Some antecedent components can also be discerned.

There are a cluster of fundamentalist traits that cross religions and cultures.[111] Martin E. Marty and R. Scott Appleby define such traits as "family resemblances".[112] Through observing similarities between radical fundamentalists in Indonesia and their Brothers with the same ideology in the Islamic world, the Middle Eastern influence appears a profound one. The complex network of ideas and world-views which radical fundamentalists from Indonesia and the Middle East hold in common, can be explained by the multifocal process of the dissemination of ideas from the Middle East to Southeast Asia. This process is grounded in age-old cross-regional and global processes of the transference of ideas. New methods of communication – such as the Internet, and physical transportation – facilitate further the general process of the globalization of Islam, including dissemination of radical fundamentalist ideas to the Indonesian archipelago.

Fundamentalism, it has been claimed, "is primarily a twentieth-century phenomenon".[113] It is true that the beginning of the current wave of radical fundamentalism in the Islamic world, including in Indonesia, dates back only three or four decades, although the fore-fathers to some of its significant tenets can be traced back to the movement of the Muslim Brothers, established in Egypt in 1928. The significant role played by ideas originating from Egypt and Saudi Arabia in inspiring radical fundamentalism in Indonesia is best con-textualized, however, by casting our analysis back beyond the twentieth century. Such a method of observation also discloses that Islamic puritanism and militancy, which are deeply grounded in Wahhabi perceptions, originated in Arabia and reached Sumatra some two hundreds years ago. In other words, the *jihad* war cry of the Padri movement preceded, by two centuries, the Holy War declared by the Wahhabi-oriented Laskar Jihad against Christians on the Maluku Islands. Similarly, it can be argued that Wahhabi per-ceptions from Arabia arrived on Indonesian soil much earlier and certainly before the arrival of Saudi petrodollars. Through a broader historical perspective, even the Laskar Jihad's request for *fatwa*s from Muslim clerics in Arabia may be contextualized in terms of the tradition of the turning of Indonesian Muslims to 'ulama in the Holy Cities, requesting legal opinions in religious matters. Consider also the prominent role played by communities of Arab descent, more precisely Hadramis (Yemenis), in radical Islamic fundamentalist groups and movements in Indonesia today. They have played a sig-nificant historical role in the proselytization of the Malay-Indonesian world from the fifteenth century on, being deeply involved in the trade between the Middle East and Southeast Asia. Today, the Hadramis are dominant among leaders of radical Muslims in Indonesia; they have a prestigious status which they enjoy as models of piety and as examples of an orthodox way of life.

Even though it is surrounded by the populated Islamic space of the Malay-Indonesian world, Singapore has appeared, during recent decades, to be almost entirely disconnected from the narrative of Islam in the region. The fact that Singapore's name has been also overtly dragged, since the end of 2001, into the case of Jama'ah Islamiyah, has caused a surprise of one sort or another. It eventuated with the arrest, mainly in Singapore, of Singaporean citizens who were alleged to be members of Jama'ah Islamiyah and with the claims that this Islamic group was plotting to attack Western targets in Singapore and even local targets. Yet, only one hundred years ago Singapore, located in a significant cross-roads of movement of people and ideas, was home to vivid Islamic thinking and activity, and even served as a regional nerve-center for the dissemination of Islamic ideas and knowledge.

An early use of the concept of *jahiliyya*, in the sense of the "modern age of ignorance", can be observed in the world-view of Persatuan Islam's activists in Indonesia. During the 1950s, preceding the current phenomenon of Islamic fundamentalism, the *jahiliyya* was used as a central ideological theme. Furthermore, one can draw a direct line from the use of the concept of *hijra* by the "Ngruki Network" in Indonesia, to a prominent forefather of Islamic radicalism, Sayyid Qutb, whose name is strongly connected with the modern reactualization of *hijra*. As Qutb's writings were translated to Indonesian, they were probably familiar to many in Indonesia. Many Indonesians are also likely to have been exposed to his ideological heritage during a common period of learning outside Indonesia. Furthermore, since Qutb enjoys the position of a significant source of inspiration for radical Muslims all over the world, it is likely that Indonesian radical fundamentalists who were trained outside of Indonesia, or interacted with various radical groups, have also been exposed to his ideas.

The concept of *hijra* also had a significant status in the ideology of the militant Darul Islam movement of West Java since the late 1940s. The reactualization of the concept of *hijra* made by

Kartosuwirjo preceded the same concept's reactualization by Sayyid Qutb, since it was only in 1949 that Qutb's first book on Islam, *al-'Adala al-Ijtim'iyya fi al-Islam* ("Social Justice in Islam"), appeared. Qutb's creative work in the preceding years was dominated by novellas, poems, and critical literary essays. Qutb once described himself in retrospect as someone who lived in *jahiliyya* for many years, making efforts to read and learn in most fields of human knowledge. It was also only at the beginning of the 1950s that he joined the Muslim Brothers; indeed, the beginning of the process of radicalization of his writings can be traced to the late 1950s.[114] Since the Darul Islam movement, and in particular Kartosuwirjo, strongly inspired the "Ngruki Network", the significance which has been given to the concept of *hijra* in the ideology of the "Ngruki Network" can be traced back to the Darul Islam movement of West Java. In 1923 the *hijra* policy of the Partai Sarekat Islam (PSI, "Muslim Association Party"), commonly known as Sarekat Islam, was launched for the first time by the Vice-President of Sarekat Islam, Hadji Agus Salim (1884–1954), during a party congress. This policy, largely motivated by a general distrust of the Dutch colonial government, could be expected to become an important part of the party's policy during the 1930s. Initially, the *hijra* policy, in the sense of a repudiation of the existing colonial structure, was closely tied to the policy of *swadeshi* ("self-help"), or non-cooperation with the colonial structure, influenced by Gandhi's non-cooperative policy in India. The policy was reviewed by the party during the 1930s by Kartosuwirjo, who had joined Sarekat Islam during the 1920s. He had a close relationship with its leader, Hajji Oemar Said Tjokroaminoto (1882–1934). He was even Tjokroaminoto's private secretary in the late 1920s. Kartosuwirjo was attracted by the combination of the policies of *hijra* and *swadeshi*. He became the chief advocate of the *hijra* policy in the party, then Partai Sarekat Islam Indonesia (PSII) when pragmatists in the party pushed its stance hard during the mid-1930s. During the robust debate in the party on this issue while serving as its Vice-President, Kartosuwirjo wrote a two-volume brochure on the *hijra* policy. This brochure would eventually lead to his expulsion from the party. In this brochure he traced the mentions of *hijra* in the *Qur'an*, and explained its meaning in each relevant context. He also argued that *hijra* is the duty of all Muslims, except the weak, and was not to be given up until real salvation and victory were attained.[115] He also stated that in almost every place in the *Qur'an* in which the word *hijra* is mentioned it is associated with *jihad.* Therefore, he argued, without the realization of the *jihad* ideal in the *hijra,* the act of *hijra* cannot be considered valid. Still, he carefully avoided an overly aggressive interpretation of the two concepts by claiming that the word *jihad* does not mean "war" in the sense in which it is often understood by Western people, but, rather, signifies sincere effort or intention to follow "the path of God, the path of Truth, the path of Reality".[116] For the same reason, he makes a distinction between *jihad al-asghar* (the "little *jihad*") and *jihad al-akbar* (the "great *jihad*"). He called to give precedence to *jihad al-akbar*, arguing that it has a constructive and positive nature at its core, and includes an element of building up, whereas *jihad al-asghar* is negative in its nature, inasmuch as it only constitutes an act of defence.[117]

Peter G. Riddell writes that scholars traditionally have tended to see Malay-Indonesian Islam as essentially derivative, since Islamic thought in the Malay-Indonesian world "has characteristically responded to pulses emanating from other parts of the Muslim world",[118] in particular the Middle East and South Asia. The previously discussed case of Islamic modernism attests, on the one hand, to the conceptually responsive nature of the Islam in the Malay-Indonesian world. But at the same time it also reveals that the ideas borrowed from the Middle East were further developed in Indonesia and were used as a platform for an Islamic reformist endeavor with its own particularities. A century before, the Padri movement in Minangkabau also emerged out of a response to a Middle Eastern stream of thought. In this case it was the Wahhabi zealous call voiced in Arabia. However, this Wahhabi response on Indonesian soil further developed into a movement which seems to be much more than simply a replica of the Middle Eastern phenomenon. The particularities of the Indonesian context also emerged in the case of the Darul Islam movement of West Java. Indeed, the current radical fundamentalism in Indonesia has a responsive nature, being largely influenced by the ideology of radical fundamentalist groups and movements in the Middle East. But also some Islamic concepts, which underwent a process of reactualization in the contemporary Islam in Indonesia, seem to be diffused into current radical fundamentalism in Indonesia.

So, through a broader historical perspective, pertaining to both the Islamic conceptual interaction between Indonesia and the Middle East and to the Indonesian local context itself, some insights which enrich the view of the complex phenomenon of radical Islamic fundamentalism in Indonesia are beginning to emerge. Observations limited to the current scene are likely to overlook some of these insights.

3
Radical Islamic Fundamentalism
The Distinctiveness of the Indonesian Context

When I travel to Syria and Iraq I feel that I see Islam's past, but when I travel to Indonesia, I feel that I see its future.

(An Iraqi intellectual, cited by Robert W. Hefner)

Marginal or Significant?

Radical Islamic fundamentalism has become a major political and social player in the Islamic world over the last thirty years. Zealous radical fundamentalists in Indonesia have shown themselves to be as destructive and extreme as their Middle Eastern counterparts. However, it seems that in comparison to a relatively significant role played by radical Islamic fundamentalism in the Middle East, North Africa, and Central and South Asia in recent decades, in the Indonesian archipelago, home to the largest Muslim community in the world, its role and position remain marginal. In Indonesia radical fundamentalist Muslims have failed to capture the imagination of the majority Muslims. They represent only a tiny proportion of the huge Muslim population in Indonesia and constitute a weak fringe and a small minority; their proclaimed goal of turning Indonesia into an Islamic state is far from realization.[1] Even Laskar Jihad, which, prior to its disbandment soon after the Bali bombings, was regarded to be the most organized Muslim militant organization in Indonesia, failed to use the local conflict on the Maluku Islands to bolster any substantial support within the mainstream Muslim community. A response of 6,000–10,000 men to its call for *jihad* against the Christians in Maluku, in the context of about 200 million Indonesian Muslims, is a relatively tiny force. The Muslim mainstream has clearly rejected the radical message of Laskar Jihad, and has not proved responsive to the attempt to play to ancient views of Christians as a threat. Laskar Jihad only gained attention and sympathy among the marginal Islamic hardliners.[2] The Islamic radical message, rhetoric, and symbols have so far revealed a lack power and have failed to be a successful mobilizing force in the Indonesian context.

Even fundamentalist positions within the established political scene appeared to be in the minority in the June 1999 elections – the first free democratic elections to the parliament, Dewan Perwakilan Rakyat (DPR, "Peoples Representative Council"), following the fall of Suharto in May 1998, and the first to be held since 1955: they are considered to provide a "litmus test for Islamic politics".[3] The optimistic expectations of many Islamic leaders of gaining over 50 percent of the votes proved hopelessly unrealistic; the Islamic political parties – those whose ideology is clearly based on Islam and who espouse several Islamic fundamentalist perceptions – gained only 16 percent of the votes. The "pluralist Islamic parties", those that, though they use Islamic symbols, have made pluralism their choice, rejected the idea of adopting the *shari'a* in the constitution and accepted the "secular"-oriented national ideology of the *Pancasila* as a sole or joint basis, gained about 22 percent of votes. The total "Islamic" vote was thus about 38 percent. The secular nationalist-oriented party of Megawati Sukarnoputri, Partai Demokrasi Indonesia-Perjuangan (PDI-P, "Indonesian Democratic Party of Struggle"), received the highest vote, almost 34 percent. Most of the voters rejected any kind of linkage between Islam and politics, and rejected the idea of an Islamic state and the Islamization of Indonesian society through the implementation of *shari'a*. The election results are regarded as additional evidence that "militant or ideologically doctrinaire Islam has rarely attracted a following in Indonesia beyond a small section of the community".[4] The decision by Majelis Permusyawaratan Rakyat (MPR, "People's Consultative Assembly"), the super-parliament constitutional body, in August 2002 to reject the proposal of Islamic parties to implement the *shari'a* for Indonesian Muslims by amending the constitution, also demonstrates this stance. The rejection of this proposal, with the strong backing of the two largest Muslim organizations, the traditionalist Nahdlatul Ulama (NU) and the modernist Muhammadiyah, also attests that radical Islamic ideals do not much hold water among mainstream Muslims in Indonesia. Indeed, the democratic experiment in Indonesia is still rather new, and patterns of voting amongst the Indonesians might undergo a process of change in the foreseeable future. Even so one cannot ignore the fact that in the recent parliamentary elections in April 2004, almost six years since the fall of Suharto, while the Western media rings alarm bells as regards the increasing threat of radical Islam in Indonesia, Golkar and PDI-P, both considered to be secular parties, are the leaders among the competing parties aspiring to the DPR, the Indonesian parliamentary body. Also in the new parliamentary composition a dominant majority of the seats, about 77 percent, will be held by these two parties together with other smaller, secular-oriented parties and with the "pluralistic Islamic parties", which clearly share with Golkar and the PDI-P the state ideology of *Pancasila*. Indeed, this time the Islamic political parties, which have Islamic political agendas, have increased, to a certain degree, their electoral share through the ballot boxes, gaining about 21 percent of the votes, which makes up 23 percent of the parliament's seats. But it must be noted that these parties, knowing that it has become increasingly difficult to "market" political Islam among Indonesian Muslims, significantly toned down their Islamic profile during the election campaign; they cautiously addressed Islamic issues and largely avoided them, went strangely silent on their vision of an Islamic state based on the *shari'a*, and most of them even did not openly advocate polygamy. Partai Keadilan Sejahtera (PKS, "Prosperous Justice Party") also proportionally topped the list of Indonesian political parties in terms of putting women as parliamentarian candidates. So, this type of Islamic parties appealed to the voters on broader issues, such as corruption and the economy.[5]

Ostensibly it is cause for wonder that radical Islamic fundamentalism has a relatively marginal position in Indonesia, since almost all the known necessary conditions for its flourishing, and almost all of its triggers we recognize in Muslim countries, exist in the Indonesian context: cultural bewilderment in a changing world and the dismantling of protective traditional institutions; a feeling of distress in increasingly alienated urban centers; economic hardships, aggravated by the ongoing effects of the 1997 economic crisis, including a high degree of unemployment; anger at the luxurious life of the elites and widespread corruption; the intensification of inter-ethnic and inter-sectarian tension and conflicts since the mid-1990s; and perhaps also some degree of political ambiguity following the current transitional period of building a new democratic polity out of previously authoritarian one.

The accumulation of similar factors in many other Muslim countries has established an appropriate setting for the emergence of radical fundamentalism. Young educated people in the Islamic world, from urban areas in particular, appear to be more receptive to radical fundamentalism. They seek to find their salvation in the simplistic answers and clearly-defined goals and messages of radical fundamentalism, which distinguish categorically between good and bad, light and darkness, heaven and hell. Radical groups provide to many people the protective haven that they seek and the feelings of solidarity and a sense of belonging that are otherwise absent. Charismatic leaders with whom they can identify are also often found in radical fundamentalism.

The Indonesian Context through a Radical Fundamentalist Prism

Hypothetical scrutiny of the Indonesian context through a radical fundamentalist filter and perceptions will find the marginal status of Islamic fundamentalism in Indonesia, and of its radical expressions in particular, a remarkable phenomenon. The Indonesian polity in its current state, in strict fundamentalist perceptions, is most likely to be considered an extremely "wrong" model that strongly opposes their own beliefs. A pivotal part of radical fundamentalist ideology is the unequivocal assertion that legitimate sovereignty belongs to God. Hence, the political order is viewed only as an earthly expression of the will of God and its rule over man. The *shari'a*, as the Divine Law, has to provide the inspiring principles for the polity. In contrast, the Indonesian state ideology, the *Pancasila*, is largely inspired by secular–nationalist ideals. As such, Islamic identity is obscured by treating equally all the recognized religions in the country – Islam, Catholicism, Protestantism, Hinduism, and Buddhism – and by keeping its first principle – Belief in One God[6] – deliberately vague. It is the *Pancasila*, with its religiously ambiguous concepts, that regulates the life of Indonesians, and not the *shari'a*. Even though Muslims are clearly predominant, representing about 87–88 percent of the population, the *shari'a* is not considered an obligatory code amongst Muslims. Through hypothetical radical fundamentalists eyes, "evils" within the way of life of Indonesian rulers could be identified. To use the radical fundamentalist vocabulary, these "evils" might be seen as signs of a "new tyranny".[7] During most of the period of the New Order, radical fundamentalists could easily point to the portrait of Suharto as the "enemy", identifying his intensive efforts since the late 1960s to limit political manifestations of Islam lest they threaten the secular foundations of Indonesia. And yet he made vigorous efforts to achieve unequivocal recognition of the established Muslim mainstream in the state ideology, *Pancasila*, as the sole foundation of the polity. In the late 1980s, Suharto shifted his Islamic policy, and he began courting Islamic circles. This included the establishment in 1990 of Ikatan Cendekiawan Muslim Se-Indonesia (ICMI, the "Association of Indonesian Muslim Intellectuals"), which would become an influential player in the political scene in the years to come. Suharto even tried to demonstrate his own Islamic piety by making a Pilgrimage to Mecca.[8] Whether it was an expression of a genuine ideological change or maneuver aimed at securing his political survival, this change of policy has strengthened the position of Islam in Indonesian society. The secular, and therefore for radical Islamists, illegitimate, *Pancasila*, however, has remained the sole ideological foundation of the state.

From a radical fundamentalist perspective, the new emerging polity in the aftermath of the fall of Suharto is also likely to be seen as "evil". Ideals that inspire this new polity, like liberal democracy,

pluralism, and human rights, are rejected by radical Islamic fundamentalism and are denounced by radicals in Indonesia. Claiming
that sovereignty belongs to God, radical fundamentalism firmly
denies popular sovereignty. Furthermore, the new polity in
Indonesia is based on the same secular–nationalist set of beliefs as
its predecessor. Likewise, the *shari'a* option is also rejected by the
new polity. Indeed, after years of strict restrictions imposed by the
government during the New Order era on political manifestations of
Islam, in the *reformasi* Muslims have been allowed to organize freely
for the first time since the late 1950s. As part of the process of
building a new Indonesian state on democratic foundations, new
Islamic parties have proliferated. Both "pluralist Islamic parties"
and Islamic political parties per se now take part in the political
process and some of their most prominent leaders include Amien
Rais, the Speaker of the MPR and Hamza Haz, the Vice-President.
But even the modern notion of a party is not acceptable to radical
Islamic fundamentalism.[9] An earlier affirmation of the Muslim
Brothers in the Middle East, which stated that only two types of
political parties exist – the "Party of God" (*Hisb Allah*) and the
"Party of Satan" (*Hisb al-Shaytan*)[10] – has often been repeated by
fundamentalists in the Islamic world, even by those that claimed to
be in favor of political participation. Also in Indonesia, the leader
of Laskar Jihad, Ja'far Umar Thalib, dubbed Christians on the
Maluku Islands as *Hisb al-Shaytan,* to justify the declaration of *jihad*
against them. Even Partai Keadilan, which later changed its name
to Partai Keadilan Sejahtera and emerged as a consequence of the
building of a democratic polity in Indonesia and hence enjoyed its
privileges, used, in its former incarnation, this dichotomy. The
profound influence of the Muslim Brothers on the ideology of Partai
Keadilan explains its stance.[11] Radical fundamentalists, including
those in Indonesia, also deny the political accommodation of
"moderate" fundamentalists who seek political participation and
accept established political rules of legitimate and constitutional
mechanisms. The particular political circumstances in Indonesia
may make political participation of the Islamic parties a difficult pill
to swallow for many radical Islamists, since the *Pancasila* is the sole
foundation of the polity and the leading political power is grounded
in the national–secular tradition. Also unacceptable from a radical

Islamic perspective is the fact that a woman, Megawati Sukarnoputri, is President of the nation. Heated debate emerged in Indonesia prior to the general elections in June 1999 over whether a woman could be president. The Wahhabi–Salafi oriented Laskar Jihad even received a *fatwa* from Saudi Salafi mufti, declaring that, "to appoint a woman as president is an act which contradicts the guidance of the Prophet".[12] The argument that a woman president was not acceptable in Islam was also repeated prior to the elections by several senior figures from Islamic parties.[13] It is unsurprising that Laskar Jihad was outspoken in its rejection of Megawati's presidency because of her gender.[14]

Through radical fundamentalist eyes it is not only the government that lives in sin, but also major segments of the Muslim community. Evil symptoms of the "modern *jahiliyya*", or the bad effects of the "sin" of modern impious civilization, would be widely identified in Indonesian society through a radical fundamentalist prism and would be severely denounced through its structure of strict beliefs and religious observance. For example, many Indonesian Muslims do not strictly observe all five religious obligations: the pronouncement of *al-shahada* (the acknowledgment that there is no divinity but that of *Allah* and that Muhammad is his messenger); the praying five times a day; the fast during the month of Ramadan; the offering *zakat* (alms); and the Pilgrimage to the holy places in Mecca. Additional "disgraceful" manners and ways of life confront Islamic radical eyes in the crowded urban centers. For example, the way that people dress and entertain themselves, the "vulgar" TV programs and films they watch as well as the ills of drug-taking, drinking, prostitution, adultery, and homosexuality. Radical Islamists usually blame rulers for this "decadent" state of affairs. Since the sovereign, according to traditional Islamic perceptions, has a religious function to defend the faith and the *shari'a*, the state is required to enable Muslims to live as good Muslims.[15] A genuine Islamic state is therefore the precondition for Muslim virtue.

Through the "globalized" prism of radical fundamentalist ideology, which gives much significance to *takfir*, the excommunication of an individual from the Islamic community, large segments of Indonesian society might be found to be either "enemies", or else "false" Muslims. Christians in Indonesia, who are regarded by radical fundamentalists in Indonesia as especially significant enemies, trigger a hostile collective memory in the minds of radical Muslims worldwide. They regard Christians as dangerous enemies of Islam, as modern embodiments of the Crusaders, and emissaries of a hostile religion. The ethnic Chinese minority is also exposed to hostile attitudes by radical Muslims in Indonesia: many Chinese are also Christians, and the one term is often used in the Indonesian context as a euphemism for the other. In addition the Hindu minority, which constitutes about 2 percent of the population, and the Buddhist minority (about one percent), many of whom are Chinese, are considered through the radical fundamentalist prism as pagans. The explosions carried out at the beginning of 1985 by radical Muslims at the significant Buddhist site, the Borobudur Temple in central Java, points to religious intolerance of Islamic Radicalism.

The millions of *abangan*, the "syncretic" Muslims, comprise the majority of Indonesia Muslims. The *santri*, the devout or orthodox Muslims, constitute a minority – no more than a third of the Muslims living in Indonesia.[16] Living mostly in rural areas, the *abangan* are deeply grounded in indigenous animism and Hindu-Buddhist traditions. The *abangan* are known as Nominal Muslims, or Statistical Muslims (*Islam Statistik*) in the sense of being Muslims for state statistics only. Therefore, through "global" radical Islamic eyes the *abangan* are likely to be viewed as Muslims in name only. The *priyayi*, the bureaucratic elite identified as having an Indic ethos, might also be viewed with suspicion, since they are regarded to be aloof from Islam in their style of life and their cultural orientations. Certain radical fundamentalists reject the widespread and deeply rooted phenomenon in Indonesia of the mystical *tarikat*s, or Sufi orders. Their profoundly unorthodox mystical perceptions and rituals are likely to be seen as heresy through the fundamentalist prism. And even though they are not part of indigenous Indonesian society, zealous radical fundamentalists will find tourists and foreigners in Indonesia to be "enemies", being "emissaries" of "sinner" civilizations and religions, which corrupt the Indonesian society, just as they have done in the Middle East and North Africa.

For the strict radical fundamentalist, Indonesia could present a major, challengeable place where those who are faithful believers and see themselves in the service of Islam are urgently required to hold back the assault of "enemies" and to defeat them. Those who are ready to fight in the name of Islam could apparently mobilize many of their members within the *umma*, the community of believers. They could easily identify through their prism "heresy", "unbelief", "false belief", "disgrace", "new tyranny", signs of "new *jahiliyya*" and as a whole host of "enemies".

With their own sense of history, radical Muslim fundamentalists who would look at Indonesia through a broader historical perspective could be also encouraged and inspired by revealing that the war cry of *jihad* has clearly marked itself through the last two hundred years. Dating back to the beginning of the nineteenth century, the Wahhabi-inspired Padri movement energetically engaged a *jihad* against the traditional *adat* order in Minangkabau in West Sumatra. The Padri movement was only defeated after a prolonged military conflict and Dutch military intervention. Furthermore, even in defeat, this movement's revivalism is considered in retrospect as a significant landmark in the history of Islamic renewal and reform in Indonesia. It also had a significant impact in the archipelago that was not limited to Minangkabau alone. There were also the peasants' revolts in Java in the nineteenth century marked, among other things, by Islamic religious revivalism and militancy. In this case anti-Western sentiments developed into an expression of hatred toward the Dutch as "infidels", conquerors, and "enemies" of Islam. The war cry of *jihad* is more clearly revealed in the Acehnese war. In 1881, the local 'ulama declared a *jihad* against the Dutch, which developed into a guerilla war inspired by Islam in an attempt to block the Dutch movement. Even though the Acehnese eventually failed after years of bitter war, their resistance was highly appreciated at the Islamic symbolic level as a significant struggle against the "infidel" colonial rule. More recently the Darul Islam rebellions, in particular the Darul Islam movement in West Java, led by Sekarmadji Maridjan Kartosuwirjo, have inspired contemporary radical Islamic fundamentalists in Indonesia. These rebellions, carried under the banner of Islam, presented a considerable challenge to the Indonesian government during the 1950s.

As to the current conflict in the Maluku Islands, it is to be primarily understood within the local context. This conflict has multi-layered origins, including ethnic, social, and economic. It also has religious aspects, but these are not the primary motivating factor.[17] As to the continuous current violent struggle in Aceh, although Islam is a significant element in the Acehnese identity, and the province of Aceh maintains an Islamic-oriented tradition of revolt dating back to the nineteenth century, the current phase of the struggle has little to do with Islam, though it is often wrongly described as an expression of Islamic radical perceptions. The conflict has many causes and driving forces, not least economic interests. Gerakan Aceh Merdeka (GAM, "Free Aceh Movement"), established in 1976, leads the struggle for independence; however it does not espouse a substantial Islamic ideology, much less radical Islamic ideals. Islam is only one element in the movement's ideology, which is largely inspired by nationalist–separatist aspirations. Hence the Indonesian government's decision in 2000 to accept in principle that implementation of the *shari'a* in the province does not have much to do with the roots of the ongoing conflict there.[18]

In the Islamic fundamentalist collective memory worldwide, the resurgence that has taken place in many Muslim countries since the end of the 1960s is regarded as encouraging. It also provides an appropriate setting for radical Muslims. The more Muslims become pious and devout believers, the easier it becomes to mobilize among them those who are ready to carry zealously the banner of Islam. Therefore, ostensibly, the Islamic resurgence in Indonesia that originated in late 1970s might have been expected to boost Islamic radical fundamentalism in Indonesia. The Islamic resurgence in Indonesia, influenced by the Islamic resurgence in the entire Islamic world, also prospered under Suharto's regime through programs of mass education implemented toward the end of the 1960s. This process brought about a dramatic increase in the literacy rate in Indonesia. As a consequence, by the early 1970s all elementary school students were receiving the same religious instruction from state-certified teachers, whereas before Suharto's New Order, most schools had implemented requirements for religious education casually, if at all.[19] Suharto also placed priority on religious education to prevent the revival of Communist ideology. Religious education increased and developed, and was incorporated into the official curriculum from elementary schools to universities.[20]

Islamic resurgence in Indonesia is more evident among *santri*-inclined communities, where more people have started observing a strictly Islamic orthodox way of life. They are more observant in daily life: praying, fasting in the month of Ramadan, paying the *zakat* and making the *hajj* to Mecca; consuming religiously approved food (*halal*); and more women are now wearing the veil. There is a growing Islamic-oriented activity on the university campuses and an intensified studying of Islam. Meanwhile the mass media have added to Islamic discourse and to the public interest in Islamic issues, and created an upsurge in the construction of mosques.[21] But at the same time a process of "*santri*-ization", or "santrification", has been included in the Islamic resurgence in Indonesia. Many syncretic Muslims, in particular among the urban middle class, have become pious and observant in their Islamic beliefs. As such they have shifted from the category of *abangan* to the definition of *santri*, moving into the mainstream tradition of Islam.[22]

Radical fundamentalists who observe the Indonesian context will be encouraged by the high potential for radical fundamentalist ideas to be diffused widely in the archipelago through varied local conduits and networks of dissemination, which include: Islamic boarding schools (*pesantren*); propagation, or *da'wa* activity, carried out by radical fundamentalist groups, including the use of modern technology to propagate their message; "study groups" (*halaqa*) on campuses, certain of which have proved to be hotbeds of fundamentalist opinions; and outstanding formative texts of radical fundamentalist thinking which been translated to Indonesian. Even political propaganda released by some Islamic political parties has the potential of inspiring radical fundamentalist perceptions.

A search of the Indonesian context for possible sources of inspiration for Islamic radical perceptions might even lead, indirectly, to the massive and influential Islamic modernist movement in Indonesia. Orthodox Muslims in Indonesia are mainly divided between modernists and traditionalists, and Islamic modernist ideas have also exerted an influence on Islamic thinking and discourse outside the confines of the modernist movement. Indeed, the Islamic modernist heritage emerged out of a sincere progressive motivation for renewal and reformation, in order to make Islam more receptive to the challenges of modernity. This objective is still maintained by the Islamic modernist movement in Indonesia, even though it has arguably lost some of its early energy and intellectual courage. But the history of Islamic modernism in the Middle East, and in Egypt in particular, has shown that, given its ambiguous character, this heritage can lead to several outcomes, and can even result in a conflict between a liberal attitude on the one hand, and Islamic–puritanical and even fundamentalist attitudes on the other. Prominent among the latter is the *salafiyya*, the puritan and pristine current of thought which was a source of inspiration for early Islamic fundamentalist movements in the Middle East since the late 1920s.[23] Even Muhammadiyah, the prominent modernist organization in Indonesia, is alleged by some to show more of a link with Rashid Rida's *Salafism* than with the original modernist ideas of 'Abduh, and to adopt a position of "neo-*Salafism*". It also must be noted that it is among modernist Muslims that many of the present-day Islamic radical organizations in Indonesia have their origins.[24] Muslim extremist voices in Indonesia are also alleged to come mostly from a modernist background; and it is rare for traditionalist Muslims in Indonesia to adopt Islamic radical positions. In the light of this, it is not at all surprising that, in the June 1999 democratic elections, the Islamist parties generally appealed to the right wing of the Islamic modernist community.[25]

The Indonesian Context: Bulwarks against Radical Fundamentalism

Having so far considered various factors of the Indonesian context, the marginality of Islamic fundamentalism in the country with the world's largest Muslim population might seem a puzzling phenomenon. But explanatory insights into the relative marginality of radical Islamic fundamentalism in Indonesia can also be found in various aspects of the Indonesian context itself. Significant is the interface between Indonesian Islam and the broader socio-political and ideological dimensions of the country.

The tradition of intellectual and organizational pluralism, which is considered to be the most distinctive quality of Indonesian Islam, is of particular importance in this regard. This quality is grounded in the tradition of religious pluralism and tolerance which exists in Indonesian society, although this tradition has often been threatened. Through *Pancasila*, the state ideology, the highly valued ideal of religious tolerance is implemented in the political scene and included in the ideological pillars of modern Indonesia. During the years that followed the struggle for Indonesian independence, and in particular during the formative discussions about state ideology and institutions, mainstream Muslim leaders and activists of political Islam expressed a desire to establish Indonesia as an Islamic state, including enforcement of the *shari'a*. But in the debate between the Islamic-oriented politicians and the leading *kebangsaan* (nationalist) group, the nationalists won.[26] As a result, Indonesia has adopted an ideology that expresses dedication to Unity in Diversity and religious pluralism. *Pancasila* respects all five dominant religions, but without giving preferential status to any one religion.

Suharto's government worked hard to anchor *Pancasila* as a dominant, inspiring ideology: a vehicle for unity, progress, and modernization. Pluralism, given the multi-faith and multicultural nature of the archipelago, had long been considered an imperative precondition. Suharto eventually succeeded in imposing the state's ideology: calls to establish an Islamic state and for the application of the *shari'a* were largely reduced during the New Order era. After the nationalist left was destroyed following the violent destruction of the Communist Party in the aftermath of the failed coup of September 1965, the regime focused on challenging political manifestations of Islam, eagerly insisting on maintaining its hegemony, not to mention its vital interest in preventing the undermining of its secular basis by political Islam. As part of the general strategy that led to the restriction of political participation and to decreasing the "space" of civil society, the regime extensively limited any political participation colored by Islam, swept away activists on campuses, and meddled in Muslim affairs. It also required large mass organizations to recognize the *Pancasila* as their "sole foundation" (*asas tunggal*). Those that refused were banned. The first Muslim mass organization to accept the *Pancasila* as its ideological foundation was the NU.[27] Despite these repressive measures, Islamic political thought did exist throughout the Suharto era. Not even the yearning for an Islamic state entirely vanished, nor the wish to see at least constitutional recognition of the Jakarta Charter from 1945, from which were removed at last moment, as already mentioned, the seven words that required Muslims to observe the *shari'a*. Active Muslims regarded the state with suspicion, considering it as embracing the idea of a secular polity and fearing its tough policy concerning Islamic political manifestations.[28]

Into this conceptual antagonism and mutual political suspicion between government and Muslim activists and thinkers in Indonesia there emerged, in the early 1970s, among the younger generation of intellectuals, a new Islamic movement, seeking an outlet from the principal ideological conflict between an Indonesian world-view (*wawasan kebangsaan*) and an Islamic world-view (*wawasan keis-laman*). The regime's highly suspicious attitude concerning Islamic political expressions, and the great difficulties Muslim activists encountered in bridging the wide gap between their theological foundations and the political reality, made it almost impossible, conceptually, to find a compromise formula between Muslim activists and the nationalists. This new young Islamic movement suggested an alternative mode of theological formulation which claimed to be attentive and relevant to the demands of the modern age and to the particularities of Indonesia. They argued for a new theological approach to *ijtihad*, the independent theological reasoning wishing to see it contextualized, to suit the contemporary circumstances of the Indonesian archipelago. In this way they aspired to make Islam more responsive to the needs of the local, temporal, and modern circumstances of Indonesia. This new approach to *ijtihad* was aimed to be an alternative to what they regarded as the overly formalist, legalist, scripturalistic orientation that characterized many Muslim political thinkers and activists. At the same time, they also expected their new theological approach to be more receptive to contemporary needs and less enmeshed in a formalist attitude than the one propagated in Indonesia by the Islamic modernist movement. One of the basic theological argu-ments of this new movement was that the holistic nature of Islam does not require a mixture between divine values and the profane state and its ideology, nor does it require that Islam should regulate every aspect of life; rather, Islam should provide moral values that serve as the basic and general guidelines for human life. Although Islam does not acknowledge the separation between the sacred domain and the profane, the two domains can, and indeed must, be differentiated. Placing these both in parallel would lead to confusion in the structure and hierarchy of Islamic values. Proponents of this trend of thought also argued that Islam does not have any particular conceptual or theoretical preferences concerning the nature of the state and its construct, or concerning its system of governing. Likewise they argued that implementation of Islam should be done culturally and that the Islamization process in Indonesia should not contradict the process of Indonesianization. Islam is complementary to the Indonesian world-view. Therefore, Islamization has to take the form of culturalization, not politicization, and Islamic movements should become cultural movements.[29]

Thus through reasoning largely based on theological and historical arguments, a creative Islamic movement that incorporates a "middle way" of Islamic political theory has emerged; a middle way that neither shared a strictly orthodox holistic perception of the state as an integral part of Islam, nor a secular perception about the complete partition between Islam and the affairs of the state. The proponents of this new movement have accepted unequivocally the current political formula of Indonesia and its structure. Some of them have even argued ardently that the existing ideological construct of the state should be regarded as a final goal or destination for Indonesian Muslims, not as a springboard for other goals or other destinations. The *Pancasila* has been presented by them as the best political formula for Indonesia. It provides an ideal blueprint for the non-sectarian identity of Indonesia that assures harmonious relations among all faiths. It also establishes a spiritual, ethical, and moral basis for Indonesia's national developments; at the same time, it guarantees freedom for Muslims to implement their religious teachings and even reflects to a certain extent the substance of Islamic principles. It therefore deserves religio-political acceptance among Muslims. This new movement even presented a case for religious–historical legitimacy of the *Pancasila* as an internal agreement that transcends religious differences. The Medina Charter was found to be appropriate for that purpose. The *Pancasila*, it was argued, ought to be regarded as similar to the

Medina Charter, the contract that was signed by the Prophet Muhammad, Jews, and the polytheists, granting Muslims the right to rule in Muhammad's city and at the same time protecting the rights of other groups. This Charter, which was initiated by the Prophet and provided basic political principles to the pluralistic society of Medina, was perceived by the new Islamic movement as an expression of Islam much more relevant to the Indonesian context, since it demonstrates a model for the relationship between Islam and politics and between Islam and the state, and realizes a genuine spirit of plurality of faith and freedom of religion in an Islamic context. Similar to the Medina Charter, the *Pancasila* expresses an accepted agreement that all shall worship none but God, without naming the state's official religion.[30]

This Islamic intellectual movement has gained considerable significance in the vivid Islamic discourse of Indonesia. Various salient terms that are part of the contemporary intellectual history of Islamic discourse during the last three decades are tightly connected with this creative movement of thought. Among them are: "desacralization", "reactualization" (*reaktualisasi*), "indige-nization",[31] "neo-modernism",[32] "Islamic liberalism" or "liberal Islam",[33] "cultural Islam",[34] and "contextual *ijtihad*" (*ijtihad kontek-stual*).[35] Three of these terms, "neo-modernism", "Islamic liberalism", and "liberal Islam" are consistently mentioned in the same breath in the Indonesian context, and perhaps best summarize the motives of this movement.

As an intellectual movement, neo-modernism is considered to be an elitist phenomenon.[36] Even so, the movement has had an impact during the last two decades on central issues and developments in Indonesia. Similarly, the prominent figures of the movement such as Nurcholish Madjid, Abdurrahman Wahid, Harun Nasution, Munawir Syadzali, Djohan Effendi, and Ahmad Wahib have acquired important positions in Indonesia's intellectual circles, influencing many young Muslim intellectuals. Their impact has crossed the confines of Islamic intellectual discourse. They have contributed to a genuine acceptance of the *Pancasila* by the Muslim mainstream as the conclusive ideological basis of the state.[37] The results of the parliamentary elections in June 1999 and in April 2004 stand as a political indicator for this. Within liberal Muslim circles, the elections in 1999 were celebrated as a victory of "cultural Islam" over political Islam.[38] On the eve of the recent elections in April 2004, a researcher from the Jakarta-based think tank, the Freedom Institute, said that Islam is not a "marketable political commodity among Indonesian voters" and that most Indonesian voters support parties with secular platforms "due to the changing culture".[39] It is likely that that neo-modernism, or liberal Islam, in Indonesia has contributed to this process, strengthening the pivotal ideals of a nation-state of pluralism, tolerance, and harmony. The liberal and progressive orientation of Islam in Indonesia toward an openness to modernity, democracy, and human rights can also be partly attributed to this dynamic intellectual movement.[40] The same may be said about the call of the movement for the use of *ijtihad* as a tool for an interpretation of Islam receptive to the needs of the modern age. Indeed, this call has been raised by the Islamic modernist movement in Indonesia since the first decades of the twentieth century as a main motif in their reformist approach, inspired by the Islamic modernist movement in the Middle East, although it has allegedly lost some of its momentum. *Ijtihad*, which stands contrary to the traditional *taqlid*, the interpretation that follows the letter strictly, is accepted by certain Islamic fundamentalists.[41] But fundamentalists definitely do not use it out of a progressive or pluralistic approach. For them it is a vehicle for providing their charismatic leaders with the right to reshape the ideals and practices of their followers. Absolute credence is given to their leaders' ruling. Given the acceptance of *ijtihad* by many mainstream Muslims in Indonesia as well, and the momentum given it by the neo-modernist movement, it is likely that fundamentalists in Indonesia are deprived of the critical argument, which is common among fundamentalists in the Middle East, about the alleged blindness of mainstream Islam to contemporary circumstances due largely to its conservative *taqlid*-oriented approach. In other words, fundamentalists in Indonesia face the challenge of a receptive and dynamic Islamic mainstream that use the concept of *ijtihad* and the idea of "reactualization" for advancing opposing ideas of their own. As a general principle, fundamentalists in the wider Islamic world are not challenged, theologically, by such an Islamic mainstream.

Since the late 1980s, the considerable contribution of neo-modernism or Islamic liberal thought in Indonesia to the building of a massive and influential civil society in general, and to the generating of the democratization process in particular, has been extremely significant. The progressive ideals of the movement are intended to act as foundations for the burgeoning civil society. Many proponents of the movement were involved in building the civil society and fortifying its ideals of social justice and human rights through the flourishing NGOs. The fact that Abdurrahman Wahid, the then charismatic leader of Nahdlatul Ulama and later to be the first democratically elected president of Indonesia, has played a leading role both in establishing this new intellectual movement and the building of civil society, clearly illustrates the close interconnection between these two spheres. The strengthening of the conceptual hold of this movement among Muslim intellectuals in Indonesia was partly facilitated by the fact that its liberal and progressive ideas are anchored in Islamic beliefs and its reasoning rooted in an Islamic context.

In the case of building a civil society and generating a process of democratization in Indonesia, one notices an unusual phenomenon: reform-minded Muslim democrats, not secular nationalists, are, since the late 1980s, the largest receptive audience for democratic and pluralistic ideals. Likewise, Muslims were the single largest constituency in the pro-democracy movement against Suharto. Voices of protest were largely raised from within Islamic organizations, groups, and movements while leading figures from the dominant Muslim mainstream in Indonesia, both traditionalists and modernists, played key roles in ousting Suharto from power. Their message was addressed toward the broader Indonesian context, expressing a desire to accomplish the ideal of building of a democratic polity in Indonesia. Mainstream Muslim commitment to democracy, constitutional law, and human rights has emerged through the years of struggle against the authoritarian regime of President Suharto and through the parallel process of shaping a civil society.[42] This process in Indonesia stands in stark contrast to the Middle East. There, the rebuff of "civil society" since the 1970s is closely connected with the Islamic resurgence in general and Islamic fundamentalism in particular, which reject secular, democratic, and pluralistic concepts of civil society. Islamic fundamentalists in the

Middle East have established large-scale voluntary associations which provide much needed economic, social, health, and education services.[43] Some sections of "pragmatic" fundamentalists in the Middle East have enlarged their borders into the dominant political scene, attempting to be accepted as legitimate political players. But their inspiring ideals and motives were quite different from those of Muslim proponents of civil society in Indonesia. In the Middle East, radical Islamists have not been inspired by democratic, liberal, and pluralistic ideals, but rather by their own notions of the Islamization of society; the state is merely a vehicle for that purpose. They rejected democratic and pluralistic ideas, even though some among them did not hesitate to use the limited opportunities of restricted "democratic" political participation for strengthening their public hold.

In Indonesia, Islamic modernism, and especially its formative and influential thinker, Muhammad 'Abduh, were significant sources of inspiration for the neo-modernist movement. This is not surprising, since Islamic modernism has a strong grasp on the Islamic mainstream in Indonesia, and exerts a considerable influence on the entire Islamic intellectual discourse therein. Both Islamic modernism and neo-modernism share the basic driving motive of making Islamic thinking receptive to the demands of modernity; both suggest that *ijtihad* is a significant theological tool for that purpose. Even the call of neo-modernist thinkers in Indonesia to a theological differentiation between the sacred and the profane can also be traced back to Muhammad 'Abduh. At the same time, neo-modernism clearly has its own distinctive merits, and in some basic aspects, like *ijtihad*, presents an even greater intellectual determination to escape the grip of strict traditional precepts.[44] Islamic modernism in Indonesia, as an earlier phenomenon, has arguably lost some of its intellectual momentum and its original ideological determination. Even so, the influence that Islamic modernism has had on neo-modernism attests to the significant role it has played in Indonesia as a source of inspiration for progressive ideas. 'Abduh's heritage has proved itself in the Middle East, and to a much lesser degree in Indonesia, to be prone to conceptual manipulation, moving away from its original progressive and reformist spirit toward fundamentalist orientations. The original voice of 'Abduh has, however, persisted in Indonesia, inspiring to different degrees

many circles in the Islamic mainstream. This conceptual phenomenon stands out as another distinctive element of Islam in Indonesia.

Also significant is the moderating role played by the two largest
Muslim organizations in Indonesia, which represent the two main
streams of domestic Islamic orthodoxy: the traditionalist Nahdlatul
Ulama (NU); and the modernist Muhammadiyah. Both have dominated Islam in Indonesia for most of the twentieth century. They are
even counted among the largest Islamic organizations in the world:
NU claims 35–40 million members, and Muhammadiyah about 30
million. The two movements share the acceptance of *Pancasila* and
the basic idea of pluralism. The traditionalist NU is regarded as
more liberal, tolerant, and comfortable with the idea of a secular
state, as well as with syncretic patterns of Islam.[45] This can be partly
explained by the fact that NU's followers are mainly from the rural
areas of Java, and as such they share the Sufi tradition of tolerance,
and are also influenced by Javanese Hindu-Buddhist and animist
traditions to a certain degree. Muhammadiyah has become more
conservative in strictly Islamic terms and there are still some people
within this movement who bid for a greater role for Islam in the
Indonesia polity. It is also possible to find among its millions of
members, and even in the ranks of the NU, individuals with a fundamentalist frame of mind who disagree with the position of the
Pancasila as the state ideology and wish to see the *shari'a* as the sole
foundation of Indonesian law. So far, however, these two movements have clearly proved themselves to be essentially moderate.[46]

Combined, the two organizations form the backbone of civil
society in Indonesia. The Muhammadiyah and Nahdlatul Ulama
constituted the only part of civil society that was to a significant
extent outside the control of Suharto's regime, since they both had
large national networks and considerable sections of the population
under their influence. A substantial number of leaders from the two
organizations were involved in pushing the government for reform.
Both of them, the NU in particular, were active in setting up NGOs
that greatly assisted in the process of the building of civil society.
Their contribution to the general well-being, by voluntarily
providing services that otherwise would not have been done by
government agencies, has proved itself to be a significant element in
building civil society. This was done through the wide network of

Muhammadiyah schools and its philanthropic institutions such as orphanages and hospitals, and through thousands of *pesantren* (Islamic boarding schools) and other charitable foundations of the NU. In 1997, during the peak of the economic crisis, Muhammadiyah and the Nahdlatul Ulama, along with a number of other NGOs, sought ways to provide food and shelter to those hardest hit. This support had a positive impact on inter-communal relations. It has been argued that there is good reason to believe that what may have prevented the sporadic outbreaks of violence from getting out of control in the late 1990s was the stabilizing effect of these two large organizations, with their extensive national networks and strong sense of community.[47]

The wide educational infrastructure of both Muhammadiyah and Nahdlatul Ulama, as well as the welfare components they possess, enables them to significantly strengthen their hold on the Muslim population and their position as the main pillars of civil society. Indeed, the Islamic radical organization, Laskar Jihad, also carried out humanitarian and communal work in the Muslim areas of the Maluku Islands and established an essential civilian infrastructure for local Muslims there. But it is clear, seen from a broader perspective, that Islamic radicals in Indonesia cannot compete with the well-established mainstream Islamic organizations. Consequently, fundamentalist groups in Indonesia do not enjoy the same privileged position that fundamentalists in the Middle East have; that is, as those who provide various services and support to large sectors of a populace deprived by the dominant regime.[48] This state of affairs has proved itself, in various areas in the Middle East, to offer fundamentalists a highly effective tool for recruiting members and gaining sympathy and popular appeal.

The nature of the Islamic resurgence, or Islamic revival, in Indonesia, is also unique. the Islamic resurgence in the Middle East and elsewhere in the Islamic world is closely connected with a growing pietism, a strengthening of Islamic conservatism and the promotion of political Islam, fundamentalist ideology, and Islamic radicalism and militancy. In opposition to this trend the Islamic resurgence in Indonesia is marked by a high degree of tolerance and general acceptance of the basic ideal of religious pluralism. Since the 1980s, the increasing interest in Islam as part of the Islamic resurgence in Indonesia has widely exposed Muslim intellectuals and many of the Muslim urban middle class to the ideals of liberal Islam, and has offered them a progressive understanding of Islam. The process of "*santri*-ization", the transition of *abangan* syncretic Muslims to the category of *santri*, or devout orthodox Muslims, which has followed Islamic resurgence, has also enlarged the circles of Muslims who adopt a liberal progressive understanding of Islam.[49] This process has been supported, at least indirectly, by another particular characteristic of the Islamic resurgence in Indonesia – an increasing interest in Sufism. The history of the expansion of Islam to Indonesia is intimately connected with Sufism, which has always had a strong influence on Islam in Indonesia. Similarly, the Islamic resurgence in Indonesia since the late 1970s has included an increasing popularity of Sufism, as Islam's "inner" (*batin*) spiritual expression. In contrast, the Islamic resurgence in the Middle East was largely scripturalist in its nature, and as such tended to avoid Sufi traditions, which are highly suspect of idolatrous accretions. Thus the mystical dimension of Islam in Indonesia has expanded beyond its traditional popular and rural space to include even the educated urban sectors. The growing popularity of Sufism is argued to be a component of the liberal neo-modernist movement[50] and the preference of the people for an independent and tolerant spirituality, as opposed to the controlled Islam of the state.[51] Thus while the Islamic resurgence in Indonesia has provided the Islamic political dimension with only a marginal role, it has enabled democratic and pluralistic ideas to establish their position within mainstream Islam in Indonesia.[52] It has also encouraged Sufism, the "Islamic spirituality",[53] which has shown itself over the centuries to support religious tolerance and pluralism.

The Suharto regime's programs of mass education, which began to be implemented toward the end of the 1960s, encouraged and accelerated the growth of the Islamic resurgence in Indonesia. This same expanding educational system was used to deliver and promote national ideals, including those of pluralism and religious tolerance. The official curriculum of religious studies, incorporated from elementary school to university, has been highly significant in this regard. A salient role has been played by the highly prestigious Institut Agama Islam Negeri (IAIN, "State Institutes of Islamic

Religion"), which was considerably expanded in Suharto's era and, what is more important, underwent a significant process of reform, changing it to a modern institution of Islamic higher education. Many of the religious teachers, Islamic intellectuals, community leaders, and Islamic functionaries in Indonesia are graduates of the IAIN, whose campuses are spread out across the Indonesian archipelago. Over the years many thousands of students have been taught at the IAIN the ideals of the state, including pluralism and religious tolerance. The curriculum has exposed them to various Islamic schools of law and theology, to other religions, and to modern sciences. It has also encouraged them, through the use of modern methods of teaching, to express freely their ideas, to be creative, and to synthesize classical Islamic studies with modern critical approaches. Likewise, the idea of using Islamic scholarship for finding solutions to modern questions is also promoted and the importance of *ijtihad* for this purpose is stressed.[54] It is not surprising that the IAIN are considered to be hotbeds for neo-modernist and liberal streams of thought and that the graduates have played a significant role in building a modern civil society in Indonesia.[55]

Summary and Reflections

The "Islamic space" in Indonesia, as a distinctive phenomenon, and in comparison to other Muslim communities, exposes its underlying features. First of all, there is a long-established tradition of religious pluralism and tolerance, regarded to be located in the foundations of Indonesian society. These ideals are among the ideological pillars of modern Indonesia anchored in the *Pancasila,* accepted by the majority of Muslims in Indonesia as the state ideology. Also conspicuous is a vivid and creative intellectual discourse and thinking toward progressive and liberal ideas of tolerance, pluralism, democracy, and human rights in the Muslim mainstream. A receptive theological approach to the demands of modernity and "cultural Islam" as a counter response to political Islam also exists. Quite distinctive is a growing civil society, highly influenced by democratic and pluralistic ideas, in which Muslims have played a formative role. Remarkable, too, is the well-established and highly influential brand of Islamic modernism that has shown itself, paradoxically, to be both a source of inspiration for progressive ideas and a point of departure for fundamentalist perceptions. A moderating role has been played by the two large and dominant Muslim organizations, the traditionalist Nahdlatul Ulama (NU), and the modernist Muhammadiyah. Both have contributed a great deal to the building of a civil society. The two organizations have developed a well-established and uncompetitive infrastructure of educational and social services that significantly strengthen their hold and appeal within the Muslim population. Also worthy of note is the distinctive nature of the Islamic resurgence in Indonesia, which is marked by a high degree of tolerance, acceptance of religious pluralism, and a growing liberal-progressive understanding of Islam. This process is supported by an increasing interest in Sufism with its historical themes of religious tolerance and pluralism, an additional particular characteristic of Islamic resurgence in Indonesia. Finally, the extensive state educational system is used as a significantly effective platform for enhancing the national ideals of pluralism, religious tolerance, and progress.

All these characteristics of the Indonesian context are integrated to provide a unique texture at the local level that has managed so far to contain radical fundamentalism, restricting it to the role of a relative marginal phenomenon. Since a difficult question obviously arises about the capacity of the local context to resist similarly radical fundamentalist ideas and positions in the years to come, some further reflections on the issue of Islam and state in Indonesia are offered.

After the fall of President Suharto in 1998, there was some ground for assuming that pent-up fundamentalist sentiments would erupt and radical elements would spread over Indonesia, a home to the largest Muslim community in the world. Six years have passed since then; time enough to argue that there is no substantial evidence to support such an assumption. Radical Islamic fundamentalism has remained on the fringes of Indonesian society. These six dramatic years have exposed the conceptual layers in the Indonesian society to reveal the profound acceptance of the *Pancasila*, the state ideology, and the democratic and pluralistic ideals within the Muslim mainstream as well as a rejection of substantial linkage between Islam and politics.

In the pluralist mosaic of the vast Indonesian archipelago, radical fundamentalism, not to mention relatively moderate expressions of fundamentalism, have a certain presence. Fundamentalist perceptions are now even expressed on the platforms of some Islamic political parties. But unlike many radical fundamentalist groups, these Islamic political parties have accepted the rules of the democratic political game and the supremacy of the state's constitution and laws. Furthermore, nowadays, due to the benefits of a democracy of the *reformasi* era, demands for a stronger position for Islam in Indonesia, including a call to establish an Islamic state based on the *shari'a*, can be expressed much more freely and clearly than under the authoritarian regime of Suharto. Even though they are fully enjoying these benefits, Islamic political parties that hold fundamentalist-oriented concepts, chose during the campaign for the parliamentary elections of April 2004 to significantly lower the Islamic profile of their original political agendas, knowing that political Islam has lost much of its attractiveness amongst the Indonesian Muslim turnout. In other words, the results of the elections do not seem to indicate that the Islamic political parties have gained more adherents for their political Islamic agenda, but rather for more general issues like improving the economy and curtailing corruption, and perhaps even for strengthening piety within Indonesian Muslims – but not for an idea of establishing Indonesia as an Islamic state.

It can be argued that the obscuring of the fundamentalist conceptions by Islamic political parties during the campaign for the parliamentary elections has to be considered as a sort of political manipulation. But one cannot entirely exclude the possibility that if this tactical approach continues, as a result of the reading of the political reality by the Islamic political parties, it might develop into a more substantial change toward a moderation of religious political positions taken by the Islamic political parties. It is important to note that the process of democratization in Indonesia is in sharp contrast to the political circumstances in many other Muslim countries, where fundamentalists are prevented from genuine political participation.

It is likely, however, that calls in Indonesia that express a wish for their society to have a stronger Islamic color will continue to be voiced in the political and public discourse there. But one cannot ignore the fact that the elections of April 2004 have provided an additional indicator to those already mentioned, that genuine fundamentalist political positions have remained a minority in Indonesia and that the concept of political Islam is largely rejected by the majority. A more recent indication of this may be the fact that both candidates who will compete on September 20, 2004 in the runoff of the first direct presidential elections in Indonesia, to determine who will lead the third largest democracy in the world for the next five years, are considered to have a secular-oriented outlook; the incumbent President Megawati Sukarnoputri and Susilo Bambang Yudhoyono, a retired general, former Coordinating Minister for Political and Security Affairs in Megawati's cabinet and the leader of newly founded party, Parati Demokrat (PD, Democratic Party).

Furthermore, the commitment of the Muslim mainstream in Indonesia to the present polity is likely to be higher than to the previous one. Since this Muslim mainstream has played a crucial role in the sweeping political changes of 1998, it is expected to identify with the democratic and liberal ideals of this new polity. For this reason, expressions of radical fundamentalist beliefs and positions that are located outside this emerging polity and do not share its ideals will continue to be considered as threat to the powerful Muslim mainstream. The shocking reminder of the Bali bombings of October 12, 2002 that killed 202 people, injuring hundreds more, and to a lesser degree some other terrorist actions, for example the lethal blast at the Marriot Hotel in the capital Jakarta on August 5, 2003, will also continue to instill in Indonesian society a feeling of being threatened by a militant strain of Islamic radical fundamentalism.

Radical Islamic fundamentalism in Indonesia, a home for a vast Muslim community, is likely to continue to be vociferous, disturbing the pluralistic and democratic polity, and creating violence and terror to achieve its ends. Indeed, although expected to remain a small minority, the radicals may cause much trouble to the dominant majority, as they are motivated by fanatical perceptions, believing absolutely in the truth of their actions, demonizing their "enemies", and enjoying some degree of operational capacity. But based on Indonesia's past and the clues offered by deeper cultural and conceptual layers of its society, it appears unlikely that radical Islamic fundamentalism, in the near future, will evolve into a real political option in the Indonesian archipelago, either by way of democratic politics, or as a political player acting outside the conventions and rules of the democratic political system. Nor does it appear poised to become a significant cultural and ideological force in the Indonesian "Islamic space".

Notes

Preface

1 Robert W. Hefner, "Islam in an Era of Nation-States: Politics and Religious Renewal in Muslim Southeast Asia", in *Islam in an Era of Nation-States: Politics and Religious Renewal in Muslim Southeast Asia*, edited by Robert W. Hefner and Patricia Horvatich (Honolulu: University of Hawai'i Press, 1997), p. 8.

2 Azyumardi Azra. *The Transmission of Islamic Reformism to Indonesia: Networks of Middle Eastern and Malay-Indonesian 'Ulama' in the Seventeenth and Eighteenth Centuries* (Ph.D. dissertation, Columbia University, 1992), p. 3.

Chapter 1 The Islamic Modernist Movement in the Malay-Indonesian World: A Comparative Look at Egypt

This chapter is a revised version of an article published by *Studia Islamika*: Giora Eliraz, "The Islamic Reformist Movement in the Malayo-Indonesian World in the First Four Decades of the Twentieth Century: Insights Gained from a Comparative Look at Egypt", *Studia Islamika*, vol. 9, no. 2 (2002), pp. 47–87.

Epigraph: William R. Roff, "Kaum Muda – Kaum Tua: Innovation and Reaction Amongst the Malays, 1900–1941", in *Papers on Malayan History*, edited by K. G. Tregonning (Singapore: Journal South-East Asian History, 1962), p. 182.

1 Fred R. von der Mehden, *Two Worlds of Islam: Interaction between Southeast Asia and the Middle East* (Gainesville: University Press of Florida, 1993), p. 13.

2 Deliar Noer, *The Modernist Muslim Movement in Indonesia: 1900–1942* (Oxford: Oxford University Press, 1978), p. 296.

3 Albert Hourani, *Arabic Thought in the Liberal Age: 1798–1939* (London: Oxford University Press, 1970), p. 161.

4 Nadav Safran, *Egypt in Search of Political Community: An Analysis of*

the Intellectual and Political Evolution of Egypt, 1904–1952 (Cambridge, MA: Harvard University Press, 1961), pp. 62–75.

5 H. A. R. Gibb, *Modern Trends in Islam* (Chicago: The University of Chicago Press, 1947), p. 34.

6 Hourani, *Arabic Thought in the Liberal Age,* p. 163.

7 Nadav, *Egypt in Search of Political Community*, p. 74.

8 Malcolm H. Kerr, *Islamic Reform: The Political and Legal Theories of Muhammad 'Abduh and Rashid Rida* (Berkeley and Los Angeles: University of California Press, 1966), p. 15.

9 Harry J. Benda, "South-East Asian Islam in the Twentieth Century", in *The Cambridge History of Islam*, vol. 2: *The Further Islamic Lands, Islamic Society and Civilization*, edited by P. M. Holt, Ann K. S. Lambton and Bernard Lewis (London: Cambridge University Press, 1970), p. 186. See also James L. Peacock, *Muslim Puritans: Reformist Psychology in Southeast Asian Islam* (Berkeley: University of California Press, 1978), pp. 19–20; von der Mehden, *Two Worlds of Islam*, p. 14.

10 See Hourani, *Arabic Thought in the Liberal Age*, p. 136; Charles C. Adams, *Islam and Modernism in Egypt: A Study of the Modern Reform Movement Inaugurated by Muhammad 'Abduh* (New York: Russel & Russel, 1968), p. 108.

11 Benda, "South-East Asian Islam in the Twentieth Century", p. 184.

12 William R. Roff, *The Origins of Malay Nationalism* (New Haven and London: Yale University Press, 1967), p. 59; Azyumardi Azra, "The Transmission of *al-Manar*'s Reformism to the Malay-Indonesian World: The Cases of *al-Imam* and *al-Munir*", *Studia Islamika*, vol. 6, no. 3 (1999), p. 82.

13 William R. Roff, "Kaum Muda – Kaum Tua", p. 166. See also Roff, *The Origins of Malay Nationalism*, p. 57; Anthony Milner, *The Invention of Politics in Colonial Malaya: Contesting Nationalism and the Expansion of the Public Sphere* (Cambridge: Cambridge University Press, 1994), pp. 168, 176; Petra Weyland, "International Muslim Networks and Islam in Singapore", *Sojourn*, vol. 5, no. 2 (1990), p. 225.

14 William R. Roff, *The Origins of Malay Nationalism*, p. 57.

15 Baroroh Baried, "Islam and the Modernization of Indonesian Women", in *Islam and Society in Southeast Asia*, edited by Taufik Abdullah and Sharon Siddique (Singapore: Institute of Southeast Asia Studies, 1986), p. 146.

16 Howard M. Federspiel, *Islam and Ideology in the Emerging Indonesian State: The Persatuan Islam (PERSIS), 1923 to 1957* (Leiden: Brill, 2001), pp. 53–61; Howard M. Federspiel, "The Muhammadijah: A

Study of an Orthodox Islamic Movement in Indonesia", *Indonesia*, 10 (1970), pp. 67–9; Noer, *The Modernist Muslim Movement in Indonesia*, pp. 80–2, 96, 302–4; Milner, *The Invention of Politics in Colonial Malaya*, pp. 176, 183–7; Roff, "Kaum Muda – Kaum Tua", p. 168; Roff, *The Origins of Malay Nationalism*, pp. 57–8; Peacock, *Muslim Puritans*, p. 18. See also M. B. Hooker, *Indonesian Islam: Social Change through Contemporary fatawa* (Crows Nest and Honolulu: Allen & Unwin and the University of Hawai'i Press, 2003), pp. 53–5.

17 Peacock, *Muslim Puritans*, p. 18. See also Federspiel, "The Muhammadijah", pp. 64–7; Noer, *The Modernist Muslim Movement in Indonesia*, p. 6, note 6.

18 Marshall G. S. Hodgson, *The Venture of Islam: Conscience and History in a World Civilization*, vol. one: *The Classical Age of Islam* (Chicago: The University of Chicago Press, 1974), pp. 238, 318, 351; Marshall G. S. Hodgson, *The Venture of Islam: Conscience and History in a World Civilization*, vol. three: *The Gunpowder Empires and Modern Times* (Chicago: The University of Chicago Press, 1974), pp. 386–94.

19 On the discussed controversial issues between the modernists and the traditionalists see John R. Bowen, "Modern Intentions: Reshaping Subjectivities in an Indonesian Muslim Society", in *Islam in an Era of Nation-States: Politics and Religious Renewal in Muslim Southeast Asia*, edited by Robert W. Hefner and Patricia Horvatich (Honolulu: University of Hawai'i Press, 1997), pp. 157–81; G. W. J. Drewes, "Indonesia Mysticism and Activism", in *Unity and Variety in Muslim Civilization*, edited by Gustav E. von Grunebaum (Chicago & London: The University of Chicago Press, 1963), p. 294; Noer, *The Modernist Muslim Movement in Indonesia*, pp. 86–7, 95, 220–1, 226; Roff, "Kaum Muda – Kaum Tua", p. 176; Roff, *The Origins of Malay Nationalism*, p. 78, note 73; Federspiel, "The Muhammadijah", p. 66; Federspiel, *Islam and Ideology in the Emerging Indonesian State*, pp. 58–9.

20 James L. Peacock, *Consciousness and Change: Symbolic Anthropology in Evolutionary Perspective* (Oxford: Basil Blackwell, 1975), p. 189.

21 Ibid., pp. 189–90; Peacock, *Muslim Puritans*, pp. 44–8, 101–11, 201; Robert W. Hefner, *Hindu Javanese: Tengger Tradition and Islam* (Princeton: Princeton University Press, 1985), pp. 104–10.

22 See Baried, "Islam and the Modernization of Indonesian Women", p. 147; M. Amien Rais, "International Islamic Movements and Their Influence upon Islamic Movement in Indonesia", *Prisma*, no. 35 (March 1985), p. 43. On the Islamic duty of *amr bil-ma'ruf wal-nahi 'an al-munkar*, see Michael Cook, *Commanding Right and Forbidding Wrong in Islamic Thought* (Cambridge: Cambridge University Press, 2000).

23 See A. H. Johns "Islam in Southeast Asia", in *The Encyclopedia of Religion*, edited by Mircea Eliade (New York: Macmillan Publishing Company, 1987), vol. 7, pp. 411–12; Roff, *The Origins of Malay Nationalism*, 58, 75–7; Roff, "Kaum Muda – Kaum Tua", pp. 167, 171, note 29; Federspiel, "The Muhammadijah", pp. 61–4; Noer, *The Modernist Muslim Movement in Indonesia*, pp. 306–7.

24 See Federspiel, "The Muhammadijah", pp. 61–4; Baried, "Islam and the Modernization of Indonesian Women"; Noer, *The Modernist Muslim Movement in Indonesia*, p. 79.

25 Fred R. von der Mehden, *Religion and Modernization in Southeast Asia* (Syracuse: Syracuse University Press, 1986), p. 90.

26 Noer, *The Modernist Muslim Movement in Indonesia*, p. 75.

27 See Drewes, "Indonesia Mysticism and Activism", p. 302; Christian Kiem, "Re-Islamization among Muslims Youth in Ternate Town, Eastern Indonesia", *Sojourn*, vol. 8, no. 1 (1993), p. 102; Noer, *The Modernist Muslim Movement in Indonesia*, pp. 75–6, 79; Mona Abaza, "The Discourse on Islamic Fundamentalism in the Middle East and Southeast Asia: A Critical Perspective", *Sojourn*, vol. 6, no. 2 (1991), p. 214.

28 See Johns, "Islam in Southeast Asia", pp. 411–12; Baried, "Islam and the Modernization of Indonesian Women", pp. 147–8; Noer, *The Modernist Muslim Movement in Indonesia*, p. 79.

29 Roff, *The Origins of Malay Nationalism*, pp. 78–9.

30 See Roff, "Kaum Muda – Kaum Tua", p. 186; Roff, *The Origins of Malay Nationalism*, p. 57.

31 Benda, "South-East Asian Islam in the Twentieth Century", p. 185.

32 Noer, *The Modernist Muslim Movement in Indonesia*, p. 306.

33 Roff, "Kaum Muda – Kaum Tua", p. 182. See also William R. Roff, *The Origins of Malay Nationalism*, pp. 86–7.

34 On the Hadrami "awakening" and its connection with the Islamic modernism, see Natalie Mobini-Kesheh, *The Hadrami Awakening: Community and Identity in the Netherlands East Indies, 1900–1942* (Ithaca: Cornell University, 1999), pp. 71–95; Natalie Mobini-Kesheh, "Islamic Modernism in Colonial Java: The al-Irshad Movement". In *Hadhrami Traders, Scholars and Statesmen in the Indian Ocean, 1750s–1960s*, edited by Ulrike Freitag and William G. Clarence-Smith (Leiden: Brill, 1997), pp. 241–5; Roff, "Kaum Muda – Kaum Tua", p. 177; Joseph Kostiner, "Impact of the Hadrami Emigrants in the East Indies on Islamic Modernism and Social Change in the Hadramawt during the 20th Century", in *Islam in Asia*, vol. II : *Southeast and East Asia*, edited by Raphael Israeli and Anthony H. Johns (Jerusalem: The

Magnes Press, 1984), pp. 214–16; Noer, *The Modernist Muslim Movement in Indonesia,* pp. 56–69.

35 Roff, "Kaum Muda – Kaum Tua", pp. 176–7.

36 Shanti Nair, *Islam in Malaysian Foreign Policy* (London and New York: Routledge, 1997), p. 16.

37 Milner, *The Invention of Politics in Colonial Malaya*, pp. 137–79.

38 Roff, "Kaum Muda – Kaum Tua", p. 183; Roff, *The Origins of Malay Nationalism*, p. 87.

39 On the modernist-oriented journals, *Seruan Azhar* and *Pilihan Timur* and on the Indonesian and Malay students in Cairo in the 1920s, see William R. Roff, "Indonesian and Malay Students in Cairo in the 1920's", *Indonesia*, 9 (1970), pp. 73–87; Roff, "Kaum Muda – Kaum Tua", pp. 183–5; Roff, *The Origins of Malay Nationalism*, pp. 87–90; Mona Abaza, *Changing Images of Three Generations of Azharites in Indonesia* (Singapore: Institute of Southeast Asian Studies, 1993), p. 3; Hussin Mutalib, *Islam in Malaysia: From Revivalism to Islamic State* (Singapore: Singapore University Press, 1993), p. 22; Noer, *The Modernist Muslim Movement in Indonesia*, pp. 153–7.

40 Roff, *The Origins of Malay Nationalism*, p. 87.

41 A. J. Stockwell, "Imperial Security and Moslem Militancy, With Special Reference to the Hertogh Riots in Singapore (December 1950)", *Journal of Southeast Asian Studies*, vol. XVII, no. 2 (1986), p. 323.

42 See Alfian, *Muhammadiyah: The Political Behavior of a Muslim Modernist Organization under Dutch Colonialism* (Yogyakarta: Gadjah Mada University Press, 1989), pp. 347–8.

43 Nair, *Islam in Malaysian Foreign Policy*, p. 16.

44 Ibid., p. 17. See also Mohamad Abu Bakar, "Islam and Nationalism in Contemporary Malay Society", in *Islam and Society in Southeast Asia*, edited by Taufik Abdullah and Sharon Siddique (Singapore: Institute of Southeast Asian Studies, 1986), pp. 156–7.

45 See Noer, *The Modernist Muslim Movement in Indonesia*, pp. 6–7, 318–19; Drewes, "Indonesia Mysticism and Activism", pp. 294–5; Alfian, *Muhammadiyah*, p. 349.

46 See Noer, *The Modernist Muslim Movement in Indonesia*, pp. 247–8, 318–19.

47 Deliar Noer prefers to use the term "religiously neutral nationalists", and argues that they were "emancipated" Indonesians who were generally Muslims and adopted a neutral and often an indifferent, if not hostile, attitude toward Islam in their struggle for independence (*The Modernist Muslim Movement in Indonesia*, p. 216).

48 Ibid., pp. 247–95, 318–21.

49 Benda, "South-East Asian Islam in the Twentieth Century", p. 187.

50 Ibid., p. 188. See also Noer, *The Modernist Muslim Movement in Indonesia*, pp. 20–9; Roff, "South-East Asian Islam in the Nineteenth Century", in *The Cambridge History of Islam*, vol. 2: *The Further Islamic Lands, Islamic Society and Civilization*, edited by P. M. Holt, Ann K. S. Lambton and Bernard Lewis (London: Cambridge University Press, 1970), pp. 180–1.

51 Noer, *The Modernist Muslim Movement in Indonesia*, pp. 162–215, 313–16. See also Roff, "South-East Asian Islam in the Nineteenth Century", p. 181; Alfian, *Muhammadiyah*, p. 342.

52 Stockwell, "Imperial Security and Moslem Militancy", pp. 323–5; Benda, "South-East Asian Islam in the Twentieth Century", pp. 186–8; Roff, "Kaum Muda – Kaum Tua", pp. 173–5; Roff, *The Origins of Malay Nationalism*, pp. 71–3.

53 Roff, *The Origins of Malay Nationalism*, p. 71; Stockwell, "Imperial Security and Moslem Militancy", p. 323.

54 See Roff, *The Origins of Malay Nationalism*, pp. 32–55, 71; Milner, *The Invention of Politics in Colonial Malaya*, p. 156; Weyland, "International Muslim Networks and Islam in Singapore", pp. 221–6.

55 Noer, *The Modernist Muslim Movement in Indonesia*, pp. 221, 316–17. See also Roff, "Kaum Muda – Kaum Tua", p. 192; N. J. Funston, "The Origins of Parti Islam Se Malaysia", *Journal of Southeast Asian Studies*, vol. VII, no. 1 (1976), p. 59; Ruth McVey, "Faith as the Outsider: Islam in Indonesian Politics" in *Islam in the Political Process*, edited by James P. Piscatori (Cambridge: Cambridge University Press, 1983), p. 216; Federspiel, "The Muhammadijah", p. 65.

56 Roff, "Kaum Muda – Kaum Tua", p. 192.

57 See Roff, "Kaum Muda – Kaum Tua", pp. 180–1.

58 See Deliar Noer, *The Modernist Muslim Movement in Indonesia*, pp. 222–34, 316; Christian Kiem, "Re-Islamization among Muslims Youth, p. 92; Benda, "South-East Asian Islam in the Twentieth Century", p. 194; McVey, "Faith as the Outsider: Islam in Indonesian Politics", p. 216.

59 Adams, *Islam and Modernism in Egypt*, pp. 70–83; Hourani, *Arabic Thought in the Liberal Age*, pp. 130–5, 143, 154–5; Safran, *Egypt in Search of Political Community*, pp. 62–3.

60 See Giora Eliraz, "The Social and Cultural Conception of Mustafa Sadiq al-Rafi'i, *Asian and African Studies*, vol. 13 (1979), pp. 101–29; Giora Eliraz, *Egyptian Intellectuals in the Face of Tradition and Change, 1919–1939* (in Hebrew) (Ph.D. dissertation, Jerusalem: The

Hebrew University of Jerusalem, 1980); Israel Gershoni and James P. Jankowski, *Egypt, Islam, and the Arabs: The Search for Egyptian Nationhood, 1900–1930* (Oxford: Oxford University Press, 1986), pp. 119, 125, 201.

61 Malcolm H. Kerr, *Islamic Reform*, p. 15.

62 M. Din Syamsuddin, *Religion and Politics in Islam: The Case of Muhammadiyah in Indonesia*'s *New Order* (Ph.D. dissertation, Los Angeles: University of California, 1991), pp. 268–70, 287–8; M. Din Syamsuddin, "The Muhammadiyah Da'wah and Allocative Politics in the New Order Indonesia", *Studia Islamika*, vol. 2, no. 2 (1995), pp. 63–4. See also Azra, "The Transmission of *al-Manar*'s Reformism", p. 97.

63 James L. Peacock, *Purifying the Faith: The Muhammadijah Movement in Indonesian Islam* (Menlo Park: The Benjamin/Cummings Publishing House, 1978), p. 24.

64 Peacock, *Purifying the Faith*, p. 6.

65 See Fred R. von der Mehden, "Islamic Resurgence in Malaysia", in *Islam and Development: Religion and Sociopolitical Change*, edited by John L. Esposito (New York: Syracuse University Press, 1980), p. 164: Fred R. von der Mehden, "The Political and Social Challenge of the Islamic Revival in Malaysia and Indonesia", *The Muslim World*, vol. LXXVI, nos. 3–4 (1986), p. 222.

66 Judith Nagata, "The New Fundamentalism; Islam in Contemporary Malaysia", *Asian Thought & Society*, vol. V, no. 14 (1980), p. 138. See also Azra, "The Transmission of *al-Manar*'s Reformism", p. 97.

67 See Alfian, *Muhammadiyah*, pp. 345–6.

68 Kerr, *Islamic Reform*, p. 15.

69 Robert W. Hefner, *Civil Islam: Muslims and Democratization in Indonesia* (Princeton and Oxford: Princeton University Press, 2000), p. 14; Robert W. Hefner, "Modernity and the Challenge of Pluralism: Some Indonesian Lessons", *Studia Islamika*, vol. 2, no. 4 (1995), p. 41; Robert W. Hefner, "Islam in an Era of Nation-States: Politics and Religious Renewal in Muslim Southeast Asia", in *Islam in an Era of Nation-States: Politics and Religious Renewal in Muslim Southeast Asia*, edited by Robert W. Hefner and Patricia Horvatich (Honolulu: University of Hawai'i Press, 1997), p. 29.

70 See Alfian, *Muhammadiyah*, pp. 346–54; Peacock, *Purifying the Faith*, p. 57; Syamsuddin, *Religion and Politics in Islam*, pp. 217–75; Ruth McVey, "Faith as the Outsider: Islam in Indonesian Politics", pp. 212–13, 217–18; Syamsuddin, "The Muhammadiyah Da'wah and Allocative Politics", pp. 35–71.

Chapter II   Radical Islamic Fundamentalism in Indonesia: Global and Local Contexts

Epigraph: Bruce B. Lawrence, *Defenders of God: The Fundamentalist Revolt against the Modern Age* (San Francisco: Harper & Row, 1989), p. 100.

1   On the "pluralist Islamic parties" see Greg Fealy, "Islamic Politics: A Rising or Declining Force?", in *Indonesia: The Uncertain Transition*, edited by Damien Kingsbury and Arief Budiman (Adelaide: Crawford House Publishing, 2001), p. 122.

2   See ICG (International Crisis Group), *Indonesia Backgrounder: How the Jemaah Islamiyah Terrorist Network Operates*, ICG Asia Report, no. 43 (Jakarta/Brussels: ICG, 12 December, 2002), pp. 3–4 (this paper can be found at the ICG website at: *http://www.crisisweb. org/projects/reports.cfm*); Rohan Gunaratna, *Inside Al Qaeda: Global Network of Terror* (New York: Columbia University Press, 2002), p. 198.

3   On Partai Keadilan Sejahtera, previously known as Partai Keadilan, see Mathias Diederich, "A Closer Look at *Dakwah* and Politics in Indonesia: The *Partai Keadilan*," *Archipel*, 64 (2002), pp. 101–15; Mitsuo Nakamura, "Prospects for Islam in post-Soeharto Indonesia", *Asia-Pacific Review*, vol. 6, no. 1 (1999), p. 104; Martin van Bruinessen, "Genealogies of Islamic Radicalism in post-Suharto Indonesia", *South East Asia Research*, vol. 10, no. 2 (2002), p. 143; Martin van Bruinessen, "Post-Suharto Muslim Engagements with Civil Society and Democracy", paper presented at the Third International Conference and Workshop "Indonesia in Transition", organized by the KNAW and Labsosio, Universitas Indonesia, August 24–28, 2003. Universitas Indonesia, Depok (see on-line at: *http://www.let.uu.nl/~martin.vanbruinessen/personal/publications/Post_Suharto_Islam_and_civil_society.htm*); Hidayat Nurwahid, & Zulkieflimansyan, "The Justice Party and Democracy: A Journey of a Thousand Miles Starts with a Single Step", in *Piety and Pragmatism: Trends in Indonesian Islamic Politics,* Special Report, edited by Amy McCreedy (Woodrow Wilson Center, Asia Program, April 2003), pp. 20–2 (see on-line at: *http://wwics.si.edu/topics/pubs/asiarpt_110.pdf*); Muhamad Ali, "The Phenomenal Rise of the Prosperous Party", *The Jakarta Post*, 20 April, 2004.

4   ICG (International Crisis Group), *Al-Qaeda in Southeast Asia: The Case of the "Ngruki Network" in Indonesia,* ICG Indonesia Briefing (Jakarta/Brussels: ICG, August 8, 2002), p. 18 (this paper can be found

at the ICG website at: *http://www.crisisweb.org/projects/reports.cfm*); ICG, *Indonesia Backgrounder*, p. 1.

5 See ICG, *Al-Qaeda in Southeast Asia*, p. 18; Greg Barton, "Assessing the Threat of Radical Islamism in Indonesia", p. 5 (see on-line at: *http://www.sisr.net/apo/Islamism_in_Indonesia.rtf*).

6 See Sadanand Dhume, "Islam Radical Appeal: Nonviolent Hizbut Tahrir is Using anti-War Sentiment to Promote Islamic Superstate", *Far Eastern Economic Review*, April 3, 2003, p. 19; ICG, *Al-Qaeda in Southeast Asia*, p. 18. On Hizb al-Tahrir al-Islami, see Amnon Cohen, *Political Parties in the West Bank under the Jordanian Regime, 1949–1967* (Ithaca and London: Cornell University Press, 1982), pp. 209–29.

7 See Gilles Kepel, *Muslim Extremism in Egypt: The Prophet and Pharaoh* (Berkeley: University of California Press, 1993), pp. 47–8; Saad Eddin Ibrahim, "Islamic Militancy as a Social Movement: The Case of Two Groups in Egypt", in *Islamic Resurgence in the Arab World*, edited by Ali E. Hillal Dessouki (New York: Praeger, 1982), p. 119; Oliver Roy, *The Failure of Political Islam* (Cambridge, MA: Harvard University Press, 1994), pp. 13, 41; Hamied N. Ansari, "The Islamic Militants in Egyptian Politics", *International Journal of Middle East Studies*, vol. 16 (1984), p. 136; Martin E. Marty and R. Scott Appleby, "Conclusions: An Interim Report on a Hypothetical Family", in *Fundamentalism Observed* (Chicago and London: The University of Chicago Press, 1991), pp. 824–5; Bahtiar Effendy, "Islam and the State in Indonesia: Munawir Sjadzali and the Development of a New Theological Underpinning of Political Islam", *Studia Islamika*, vol. 2, no. 2 (1995), p. 111; R. Hrair Dekmejian, *Islam in Revolution: Fundamentalism in the Arab World* (New York: Syracuse University Press, 1985), pp. 90–3.

8 See ICG, *Al-Qaeda in Southeast Asia*, p. 7.

9 On Jakarta Charter, see: Hyung-Jun Kim, "The Changing Interpretation of Religious Freedom in Indonesia", *Journal of Southeast Asian Studies*, vol. 29, no. 2 (1998), pp. 357–73. See also ICG (International Crisis Group), *Indonesia: Violence and Radical Muslims*, ICG Indonesia Briefing (Jakarta/Brussels: ICG, October 10, 2001), pp. 11, 14–15 (this paper can be found at the ICG website at: *http://www.crisisweb.org/projects/reports.cfm*); van Bruinessen, "Genealogies", p. 120.

10 Majid Khadduri, *War and Peace in the Law of Islam* (Baltimore: The Johns Hopkins Press, 1955), pp. 55–73.

11 R. Hrair Dekmejian, *Islam in Revolution*, p. 45; See also E. Tyan,

"Djihad", in *The Encyclopaedia of Islam*, new edition, edited by B. Lewis, Ch. Pellat and J. Schacht (Leiden: E.J. Brill and London: Luzac & Co., 1965), p. 538.

12   See Noorhaidi, Hasan, "Faith and Politics: The Rise of The Laskar Jihad in The Era of Transition in Indonesia, *Indonesia*, 73 (April 2002), pp. 165–9; Grag Barton, "The Prospects for Islam", in *Indonesia Today: Challenges of History*, edited by Grayson Lloyd and Shannon Smith (Singapore: Institute of Southeast Asian Studies, 2001), pp. 247–9, 253–4; Greg Fealy, "Inside Laskar Jihad: An Interview with the Leader of a New Radical and Militant Sect", *Inside Indonesia*, no. 65, January–March 2001, pp. 28–9; Badrus Sholeh, "Islamic Forces in Maluku". Unpublished paper presented at workshop on "The Dynamics of Political Islam in Indonesia", organized by Melbourne University and Melbourne Indonesia Consortium Conference (Melbourne, July 2003); Text of "Declaration of War" by the Leader of Laskar Jihad, BBC Monitoring International Reports (see on-line at: *http://www.websitesrcg.com/ambon/documents/laskar-jihad-010502. htm*).

13   Hasan, "Faith and Politics", pp. 165–7; Rohan Gunaratna, *Inside Al Qaeda*, pp. 201–2.

14   See Muhammad Umar As-Sewed, "Musuh", *Buletin Laskar Jihad Ahlus Sunnah wal Jamaah*, 10, Tahun I (2001), p. 3; Adian Husaini, "Makna Jihad", *Buletin Laskar Jihad Ahlus Sunnah wal Jamaah*, 13, Tahun I (2001), pp. 4–5.

15   See R. Hrair Dekmejian, *Islam in Revolution*, pp. 47–9, 90–3.

16   Hasan, "Faith and Politics", p. 167. See also Sholeh, "Islamic Forces in Maluku", p. 8; Michael Davis, "Laskar Jihad and the Political Position of Conservative Islam in Indonesia", *Contemporary Southeast Asia*, vol. 24, no. 1 (April 2002), p. 24.

17   See ICG, *Indonesia: Violence and Radical Muslims*, pp. 7–8; van Bruinessen, "Genealogies", p. 146.

18   Marty and Appleby, "Conclusions", pp. 820–1.

19   See Bruce B. Lawrence, *Defenders of God: The Fundamentalist Revolt against the Modern Age* (San Francisco: Harper & Row, 1989), p. 100.

20   See Ja'far Umar Thalib, "Makar", *Buletin Laskar Jihad Ahlus Sunnah wal Jamaah*, 5, Tahun I (2001), p. 6; Ja'far Umar Thalib, "Merapikan Barisan Muslimin Menghadapi Permusuhan Salibis dan Zionis International", *Buletin Laskar Jihad Ahlus Sunnah wal Jamaah*, 25, Tahun II (4–17 Oktober 2002), pp. 4–5; Ja'far Umar Thalib, "Munafiq", *Buletin Laskar Jihad Ahlus Sunnah wal Jamaah*, 6, Tahun I (2001), p. 7; Dzulqarnain, "Rahmat Islam di Medan Tempur",

Salafy, 36 (2001), pp. 19–21; Dzulqarnain bin Muhammad Al-Atsari, "Rahmat Islam Terhadap Orang Kafir", *Salafy*, 36 (2001), pp. 24–30; Muhammad Umar As-Sewed, "Musuh", p. 3; Muhammad Umar As-Sewed, "Sabar dalam Jihad", *Buletin Laskar Jihad Ahlus Sunnah wal Jamaah*, 15, Tahun I (2002), p. 3; Muhammad Umar As-Sewed, "Terorisme adalah Budaya Kafir", *Buletin Laskar Jihad Ahlus Sunnah wal Jamaah*, 23, Tahun II (August 2002), p. 3; Abu Usamah Abdurrahman Ibnu Rawiyah An-Nawawi, "Berlindung dari Fitnah Syirik Kufur & Munafik", *Salafy*, 36 (2001), pp. 42–4; Greg Fealy, "Inside Laskar Jihad", pp. 28–9; Transcript of Abu Bakar's Comment, December 13, 2002 (see on-line at: *http://smh.com.au/articles/2002/12/13/1039656177555.html*); Text of "Declaration of War" by the leader of Laskar Jihad.

21 See Noorhaidi Hasan, "Faith and Politics: The Rise of The Laskar Jihad in the Era of Transition in Indonesia", *Indonesia*, 73 (April 2002), pp. 152–3.

22 See Emmanuel Sivan, *Radical Islam: Medieval Theology and Modern Politics*, enlarged edition (New Haven and London: Yale University Press, 1990), pp. 21–35; Kepel, *Muslim Extremism in Egypt*, pp. 13, 36–59; Ibrahim, "Islamic Militancy as a Social Movement", p. 121; Roy, *The Failure of Political Islam*, pp. 41, 73, 95, 99–100; John O. Voll, "Fundamentalism in the Sunni Arab World: Egypt and the Sudan", in *Fundamentalism Observed*, edited by Martin E. Marty and R. Scott Appleby (Chicago and London: The University of Chicago Press, 1991), pp. 371–2; Olivier Carré, *Mysticism and Politics: A Critical Reading of Fi Zilal al-Qur'an by Sayyid Qutb (1906–1966)*, translated from French by Carol Artigues and revised by W. Shepard (Leiden: Brill, 2003), pp. 307–21; Hamid Algar, in the introduction to Sayyid Qutb, *Social Justice in Islam*, translated from the Arabic by John B. Hardie. Translation revised and introduction by Hamid Algar (Oneonta: Islamic Publications International, 2000), p. 8.

23 ICG, *Indonesia Backgrounder*, p. 22.

24 See Fachry Ali and Bahtiar Effendy, *Merambah Jalan Baru Islam: Rekonstruksi Pemikiran Islam Indonesia Masa Orde Baru* (Bandung: Mizan, 1986), pp. 268–77; M. Din Syamsudin, "Islamic Political Thought and Cultural Revival in Modern Indonesia", *Studia Islamika*, vol. 2, no. 4 (1995), p. 59; Bahtiar Effendy, *Islam and the State in Indonesia* (Singapore: Institute of Southeast Asian Studies, 2003), p. 105; Effendy, "Islam and the State in Indonesia", p. 112; Fred R. von der Mehden, *Two Worlds of Islam: Interaction between Southeast Asia and the Middle East* (Gainesville: University Press of

Florida, 1993), pp. 74, 76–7, 87–8, 91; M. Dawam Rahardgo, "Perceptions of Culture in the Islamic Movement: An Indonesian Perspective", *Sojourn*, vol. 7, no. 2 (August 1992), p. 256; Mona Abaza, "The Discourse on Islamic Fundamentalism in the Middle East and Southeast Asia: A Critical Perspective", *Sojourn*, vol. 6, no. 2 (August 1991), p. 215; Mona Abaza, *Changing Images of Three Generations of Azharites in Indonesia* (Singapore: Institute of Southeast Asian Studies, 1993), pp. 5–6; Dini Djalal, "The Past Catches Up", *Far Eastern Economic Review*, November 14, 2002; van Bruinessen, "Genealogies", pp. 125–6, 149.

25 See Qutb, Sayid, *Petunjuk Jalan*, alih bahasa, A. Rahman Zainuddin (Jakarta: Media Dakwah, 1980).

26 See Voll, "Fundamentalism in the Sunni Arab World", pp. 368–74.

27 Howard M. Federspiel, *Islam and Ideology in the Emerging Indonesian State: The Persatuan Islam (PERSIS), 1923 to 1957* (Leiden: Brill, 2001), pp. 244–5, 272, 325–6.

28 Voll, "Fundamentalism in the Sunni Arab World", p. 372. See also Marty and Appleby, "Conclusions", p. 821; Dekmejian, *Islam in Revolution*, p. 92.

29 See Reuven Paz, "Global Jihad and the United States: Interpretation of the New World Order of Usama Bin Ladin", *PRISM Series of Global Jihad*, no. 1, February 2003 (see on-line at: *http://gloria.idc.ac.il /islam/global_jihad.html*).

30 ICG, *Al-Qaeda in Southeast Asia*, pp. 7, 11–13, 15. See also ICG, *Indonesia Backgrounder*, p. 3; Rohan Gunaratna, *Inside Al Qaeda*, p. 198.

31 See Ibrahim Abu Rabi', "Christian-Muslim Relations in Indonesia: The Challenges of the Twenty-First Century", *Studia Islamika*, vol. 5, no. 1 (1998), p. 8; Deliar Noer, "Contemporary Political Dimensions of Islam", in *Islam in South-East Asia*, edited by M. B. Hooker (Leiden: E.J. Brill, 1983), p. 197; ICG, *Indonesia: Violence and Radical Muslims*, p. 14; van Bruinessen, "Genealogies", p. 123; R. William Liddle, "*Media Dakwah* Scripturalism: One Form of Islamic Political Thought and Action in New Order Indonesia, in *Toward a New Paradigm: Recent Developments in Indonesian Islamic Thought*, edited by Mark R. Woodward (Tempe: Arizona State University, Program for Southeast Asian Studies, 1996), p. 330.

32 On the term *harbi*, see Khadduri, *War and Peace in the Law of Islam*, pp. 163, 165–6.

33 Fealy, "Inside Laskar Jihad", pp. 28–9. See also As-Sewed, "Terorisme adalah Budaya Kafir", p. 3; Hasan, "Faith and Politics", p. 167.

34 See Adam Schwarz, *A Nation in Waiting: Indonesia's Search for Stability*, 2nd edition (Boulder, CO: Westview Press, 2000), p. 331.

35 Greg Barton, " Islam and Politics in the New Indonesia", in *Islam in Asia*, edited by Jason F. Isaacson and Colin Rubenstein (New Brunswick: Transaction Publishers, 2002), p. 3.

36 ICG, *Indonesia: Violence and Radical Muslims*, p.6.

37 See ibid., p. 9; Hasan, "Faith and Politics", pp. 161, 164.

38 Duglas E. Ramage, *Politics in Indonesia: Democracy, Islam and the Ideology of Tolerance*, London: Routledge, 1997, pp. 23–4; see also M. C. Ricklefs, *A History of Modern Indonesia: Since c. 1200*, 3rd edition (Stanford: Stanford University Press, 2001), 312–43.

39 See Tim Behrend, "Preaching Fundamentalism: The Public Teachings of Abu Bakar Ba'asyir", *Inside Indonesia*, no. 74 (April–June 2003), p. 10.

40 See ICG, *Indonesia: Violence and Radical Muslims*, p. 14.

41 See Ja'far Umar Thalib, pp. 4–5; As-Sewed, "Sabar dalam Jihad", p. 3; Hasan, "Faith and Politics", pp. 161, 163–5; Transcript of Abu Bakar's Comment; Text of "Declaration of War" by the leader of Laskar Jihad.

42 See Liddle, "*Media Dakwah* Scripturalism", pp. 328–35; Barton, "Islam and Politics in the New Indonesia", pp. 37–8; 49–51, 56–9; Barton, "The Prospects for Islam", pp. 248, 250–1; Barton, *Assessing the Threat of Radical Islamism in Indonesia*, p. 12–13; Schwarz, *A Nation in Waiting*, pp. 330–1.

43 See van Bruinessen, "Genealogies", p. 118.

44 See Liddle, "*Media Dakwah* Scripturalism", p. 328; Barton, "Islam and Politics in the New Indonesia", pp. 49–50; Schwarz, *A Nation in Waiting: Indonesia's Search for Stability*, pp. 330–1.

45 Robert W. Hefner, "Print Islam: Mass Media and Ideological Rivalries among Indonesian Muslims", *Indonesia*, 64 (October 1997), p. 86. See also van Bruinessen, "Genealogies", pp. 123, 127.

46 See ibid., pp. 125–6; von der Mehden, *Two Worlds of Islam*, p. 91.

47 van Bruinessen, "Genealogies", p.134.

48 Hasan, "Faith and Politics", pp. 151–62. See also van Bruinessen, "Genealogies", pp. 134, 144–5; Robert W. Hefner, "Civic Pluralism Denied? The New Media and *Jihadi* Violence in Indonesia", in *New Media in the Muslim World*, edited by Dale F. Eickelman, 2nd edition (Indiana University Press, 2003).

49 Hasan, "Faith and Politics", pp. 151–2.

50 See Djalal, "The Past Catches Up".

51 See M. Amien Rais, "International Islamic Movements and their

Influence upon Islamic Movements in Indonesia", *Prisma*, no. 35 (March 1985), pp. 46–7; M. Din Syamsuddin, "Islamic Political Thought and Cultural Revival in Modern Indonesia", p. 62; von der Mehden, *Two Worlds of Islam,* pp. 74, 86–8.

52 ICG, *Al-Qaeda in Southeast Asia*, p.10; van Bruinessen, "Genealogies", p. 133.

53 von der Mehden, *Two Worlds of Islam*, p. 97.

54 Ibid., pp. xii, 73–4, 87–9, 91, 97; van Bruinessen, "Genealogies", pp. 126–7, 131, 149. See also Feener R. Michael, *Developments of Muslim Jurisprudence in Twentieth Century Indonesia* (Ph.D. dissertation, Boston: Boston University, 1999), pp. 191–5, 245–6. Mark R. Woodward, "Conversations with Abdurrahman Wahid", in *Toward a New Paradigm: Recent Developments in Indonesian Islamic Thought*, edited by Mark R. Woodward (Tempe: Arizona State University, Program for Southeast Asian Studies, 1996), p. 148; *Al-Qaeda in Southeast Asia*, pp. 8–10.

55 On Laskar Jihad and the new media see Robert W. Hefner, "Civic Pluralism Denied?"

56 See ICG, *Indonesia: Violence and Radical Muslims*, p. 12; ICG, *Al-Qaeda in Southeast Asia*, p. 6; Djalal, "The Past Catches Up", pp. 16–19; van Bruinessen, "Genealogies", pp. 145, 148; Hasan, "Faith and Politics", p. 151.

57 See Barbara Watson Andaya and Yoneo Ishii, "Religious Developments in Southeast Asia, *c.* 1500–1800", in *The Cambridge History of Southeast Asia*, vol. one: *From Early Times to c. 1800*, edited by Nicholas Tarling (Cambridge: Cambridge University Press, 1992), pp. 513–27; Drewes, G. W. J., "New Light on the Coming of Islam to Indonesia?", in *The Propagation of Islam in the Indonesian-Malay Archipelago*, edited and annotated by Alijah Gordon (Kuala Lumpur: Malaysian Sociological Research Institute, 2001), pp. 125–55; A. H. Johns, "Islam in Southeast Asia" in *The Encyclopedia of Religion*, edited by Mircea Eliade (New York: Macmillan Publishing Company, 1987), vol. 7, pp. 406–9; M. C. Ricklefs, "Six Centuries of Islamization in Java, in *Conversion to Islam*, edited by Nehemia Levtzion (New York: Holmes & Meier Publishers, Inc., 1979), pp. 100–12.

58 William R. Roff, *The Origins of Malay Nationalism* (New Haven and London: Yale University Press, 1967), pp. 39–43; Natalie Mobini-Kesheh, *The Hadrami Awakening: Community and Identity in the Netherlands East Indies, 1900–1942* (Ithaca: Cornell University, 1999), p. 21; Peter G. Riddell, "Religious Links between Hadramaut and the Malay-Indonesian World, *c.* 1850 to *c.* 1950", in *Hadrami Traders,*

Scholars and Statesmen in the Indian Ocean, 1750s–1960s, edited by Ulrike Freitag and William G. Clarence-Smith (Leiden: Brill, 1997), p. 221.

59　See R. A. Kern, "The Propagation of Islam in the Indonesian-Malay Archipelago" (translated by H. M. Froger and annotated by Alijah Gordon), in *The Propagation of Islam in the Indonesian-Malay Archipelago*, edited and annotated by Alijah Gordon (Kuala Lumpur: Malaysian Sociological Research Institute, 2001), pp. 85–6.

60　Mark R. Woodward, *Islam in Java: Normative Piety and Mysticism in the Sultanate of Yogyakarta* (Tucson: The University of Arizona Press, 1989), p. 244.

61　William R. Roff, "South-East Asian Islam in the Nineteenth Century", in *The Cambridge History of Islam*, vol. 2: *The Further Islamic Lands, Islamic Society and Civilization*, edited by P. M. Holt, Ann K. S. Lambton and Bernard Lewis (London: Cambridge University Press), pp. 180–1; Roff, *The Origins of Malay Nationalism*, p. 39; von der Mehden, *Two Worlds of Islam*, p. 3; Robert W. Hefner, *Civil Islam: Muslims and Democratization in Indonesia* (Princeton and Oxford: Princeton University Press, 2000), p. 32.

62　See C. van Dijk, "Colonial Fears, 1890–1918: Pan-Islamism and the Germano-Indian Plot, in *Transcending Borders: Arabs, Politics, Trade and Islam in Southeast Asia*, edited by Huub De Jonge and Nico Kaptein (Leiden: KITLV Press: 2002), pp. 53–89; Huub de Jonge, "Dutch Colonial Policy pertaining to Hadrami Immigrants", in *Hadrami Traders, Scholars and Statesmen in the Indian Ocean, 1750s–1960s*, edited by Ulrike Freitag and William G. Clarence-Smith (Leiden: Brill, 1997), pp. 106–11.

63　See Peter G. Riddell, "Arab Migrants and Islamization in the Malay World during the Colonial Period", *Indonesia and the Malay World*, vol. 29, no. 84 (2001), pp. 115–16.

64　von der Mehden, *Two Worlds of Islam*, p. 3. See also Sartono Kartodirdjo, *The Peasant's Revolt of Banten in 1888: Its Conditions, Course and Sequel: A Case Study of Social Movements in Indonesia* ('s-Gravenhage: Martinus Nijhoff, 1966), p. 143.

65　See A. C. Milner, "Islam and the Muslim State", in *Islam in South-East Asia*, edited by M. B. Hooker (Leiden: E.J. Brill, 1983), pp. 45–9.

66　Roff, "South-East Asian Islam in the Nineteenth Century", p. 169.

67　Deliar Noer, *The Modernist Muslim Movement in Indonesia: 1900–1942* (Oxford: Oxford University Press, 1978), p. 29.

68　Harry J. Benda, "South-East Asian Islam in the Twentieth Century", in *The Cambridge History of Islam*, vol. 2: *The Further Islamic Lands,*

Islamic Society and Civilization, edited by P. M. Holt, Ann K. S. Lambton and Bernard Lewis (London: Cambridge University Press, 1970), p. 182. See also von der Mehden, *Two Worlds of Islam*, p. 4; Anthony Reid, "Introduction", in *The Making of an Islamic Political Discourse in Southeast Asia*, edited by Anthony Reid (Monash Papers on Southeast Asia – no. 27, Clayton: Monash University, 1993), p. 9.

69 See Peter G. Riddell, *Islam and the Malay-Indonesian World: Transmission and Responses* (Honolulu: University of Hawai'i Press, 2001), pp. 8–9.

70 M. F. Laffan, *Islamic Nationhood and Colonial Indonesia: The Umma Below the Winds* (London and New York: RoutledgeCurzon, 2003), 20.

71 Ibid., p. 13.

72 On the *jawa* community in Arabia see Azyumaidi Azra, *The Transmission of Islamic Reform to Indonesia: Networks of Middle Eastern and Malay-Indonesian 'Ulama' in the Seventeenth and Eighteenth Century* (Ph.D. dissertation, Columbia University, 1992); Laffan, *Islamic Nationhood and Colonial Indonesia*; Riddell, *Islam and the Malay-Indonesian World*, pp. 8–9; Riddell, "Arab Migrants and Islamization in the Malay World during the Colonial Period", p. 116; Roff, *The Origins of Malay Nationalism*, p. 45; Roff, "South-East Asian Islam in the Nineteenth Century", pp. 172–3; von der Mehden, *Two Worlds of Islam*, p. 13; C. Snouck Hurgronje, *Mekka in the Latter Part of the 19th Century: Daily Life, Customs and Learning the Moslims of the East-Indian-Archipelago*, translated by J. H. Monahan (Leiden: E.J. Brill, 1970), p. 215; Nico Kaptein, "Meccan Fatwas from the End of the Nineteenth Century on Indonesia Affairs", *Studia Islamika*, vol. 2, no. 4 (1995), pp. 141–60.

73 See Riddell, *Islam and the Malay-Indonesian World*, p. 9.

74 See Martin van Bruinessen, "Muslims of the Dutch East Indies and the Caliphate Question, *Studia Islamika*, vol. 2, no. 3, pp. 115–40; von der Mehden, *Two Worlds of Islam*, pp. 10–12.

75 William R. Roff, "Indonesian and Malay Students in Cairo in the 1920's", *Indonesia*, 9 (1970), p. 74.

76 Abaza, *Changing Images of Three Generations of Azharites in Indonesia*; von der Mehden, *Two Worlds of Islam*, pp. 91–4; Mona Abaza, "Some Research Notes on Living Conditions and Perceptions Among Indonesian Students in Cairo", *Journal of Southeast Asia Studies*, vol. 22, no. 2 (September 1991), pp. 356–7.

77 See Hefner, "Print Islam, p. 86; Abaza, "Some Research Notes on Living Conditions and Perceptions Among Indonesians Students in Cairo", p. 359; von der Mehden, *Two Worlds of Islam*, pp. 90, 93.

‖ 109 ‖

78 See Mona Abaza, "Indonesian Azharities, Fifteen Years Later", *Sojourn*, vol. 18, no. 1 (2003), pp. 139–53.
79 See Syed Farid Alatas, "Hadhramaut and the Hadhrami Diaspora: Problems in Theoretical History", in *Hadhrami Traders, Scholars and Statesmen in the Indian Ocean, 1750s–1960s*, edited by Ulrike Freitag and William G. Clarence-Smith (Leiden: Brill, 1997), pp. 29–31.
80 See Natalie Mobini-Kesheh, *The Hadrami Awakening: Community and Identity in the Netherlands East Indies, 1900–1942* (Ithaca: Cornell University, 1999), p. 21.
81 Huub de Jonge and Nico Kaptein Engseng, "The Arab Presence in Southeast Asia: Some Introductory Remarks", in *Transcending Borders: Arabs, Politics, Trade and Islam in Southeast Asia*, edited by Huub De Jonge and Nico Kaptein (Leiden: KITLV Press: 2002), p. 2.
82 Ibid.
83 William G. Clarence-Smith, "Hadramaut and the Hadrami Diaspora in the Modern Colonial Era: An Introductory Survey", in *Hadhrami Traders, Scholars and Statesmen in the Indian Ocean, 1750s–1960s*, edited by Ulrike Freitag and William G. Clarence-Smith (Leiden: Brill, 1997), p. 5; Mobini-Kesheh, *The Hadrami Awakening*, p. 21; Roff, *The Origins of Malay Nationalism*, p. 40.
84 On the role of the Hadramis as cultural brokers between the Middle East and the Malay-Indonesian world, see Mobini-Kesheh, *The Hadrami Awakening*; Riddell, "Arab Migrants and Islamization in the Malay World during the Colonial Period", pp. 114–19, 122–3; Riddell, "Religious Links between Hadramaut and the Malay-Indonesian World", pp. 217–30; Noer, pp. 56–69; Roff, *The Origins of Malay Nationalism*, pp. 39–43; Joseph Kostiner, "Impact of the Hadrami Emigrants in the East Indies on Islamic Modernism and Social Change in the Hadramawi during the 20th Century" in *Islam in Asia*, vol. II: *Southeast and East Asia*, edited by Raphael Israeli and Anthony H. Johns (Jerusalem: The Magnes Press, 1984), pp. 206–11; Federspiel, *Islam and Ideology in the Emerging Indonesian State*, pp. 59–60.
85 See Mobini-Kesheh, *The Hadrami Awakening*, pp. 34–127.
86 Huub de Gonge," Dutch Colonial Policy pertaining to Hadhrami Immigrants" in *Hadhrami Traders, Scholars and Statesmen in the Indian Ocean, 1750s–1960s*, edited by Ulrike Freitag and William G. Clarence-Smith (Leiden: Brill, 1997), pp. 94–111; Sumit K. Mandal, "Natural Leaders of Native Muslims: Arab Ethnicity and Politics in Java under Dutch Rule", in *Hadhrami Traders, Scholars and Statesmen in the Indian Ocean, 1750s–1960s*, edited by Ulrike Freitag and William G. Clarence-Smith (Leiden: Brill, 1997), pp. 185–98; Sumit K. Mandal,

"Forging a Modern Arab Identity in Java in the Early Twentieth Century", in *Transcending Borders: Arabs, Politics, Trade and Islam in Southeast Asia*, edited by Huub De Jonge and Nico Kaptein (Leiden: KITLV Press, 2002), pp. 163–84; van Dijk, "Colonial Fears, 1890–1918", pp. 53–89.

87 Huub de Gonge," Dutch Colonial Policy pertaining to Hadhrami Immigrants", pp. 106–11.

88 Federspiel, *Islam and Ideology in the Emerging Indonesian State*, p. 8.

89 Mandel, " Forging a Modern Arab Identity in Java", pp. 172–6.

90 Mobini-Kesheh, *The Hadrami Awakening*, pp. 52, 75.

91 Mandel, "Forging a Modern Arab Identity in Java", pp. 172–6.

92 Jutta E. Bluhm, "A Preliminary Statement on the Dialogue Established between the Reform Magazine *al-Manar* and the Malayo-Indonesian World", *Indonesia Circle*, no. 32 (November 1983), pp. 35–42; Riddell, *Islam and the Malay-Indonesian World*, pp. 208–10; Moch Nur Ichwan, "Differing Responses to an Ahmadi Translation and Exegesis: The Holy *Qur'an* in Egypt and Indonesia", *Archipel*, 62 (2001), pp. 148–50; William R. Roff, "Kaum Muda – Kaum Tua: Innovation and Reaction Amongst the Malays, 1900–1941", in *Papers on Malayan History*, edited by K. G. Tregonning (Singapore: Journal South-East Asian History,1962), p. 172 note 31; Roff, *The Origins of Malay Nationalism*, pp. 56–67; Azyumardi Azra, "The Transmission of al-*Manar*'s Reformism to the Malay-Indonesian World: The Cases of *al-Imam* and *al-Munir*", *Studia Islamika*, vol. 6, no. 3 (1999), pp. 79–97. On al-*Imam* see also Anthony Milner, *The Invention of Politics in Colonial Malaya: Contesting Nationalism and the Expansion of the Public Sphere* (Cambridge: Cambridge University Press, 1994), pp. 137–66.

93 See Noer, *The Modernist Muslim Movement in Indonesia*, pp. 56–7. About al-'Urwa al-Wuthqa see Albert Hourani, *Arabic Thought in the Liberal Age: 1798–1939* (London: Oxford University Press, 1970), pp. 109–10.

94 Roff, *The Origins of Malay Nationalism*, p. 50.

95 For list of these Arabic newspapers, see William R. Roff, *Bibliography of Malay and Arabic Periodicals Published in the Straits Settlements and Peninsular Malay States, 1876–1941* (London: Oxford University Press, 1972), pp. 59–61.

96 von der Mehden, *Two Worlds of Islam*, p. 6.

97 Roff, *The Origins of Malay Nationalism*, pp. 32–55; William R. Roff, "Murder as an Aid to Social History: The Arabs in Singapore in the Early Twentieth Century", in *Transcending Borders: Arabs, Politics,*

Trade and Islam in Southeast Asia, edited by Huub De Jonge and Nico Kaptein (Leiden: KITLV Press: 2002), p. 91.

98 See Roff, *The Origins of Malay Nationalism*, pp. 32–55; von der Mehden, *Two Worlds of Islam*, p. 13; Roff, "South-East Asian Islam in the Nineteenth Century", p. 177; Benda, "South-East Asian Islam in the Twentieth Century", p. 184; Riddell, "Arab Migrants and Islamization in the Malay World during the Colonial Period", p. 116.

99 Watson and Ishii, "Religious Developments in Southeast Asia", p. 520.

100 Abaza, *Changing Images of Three Generations of Azharites in Indonesia*, p. 13. See also ibid., pp. 14–18; Abaza, "Indonesian Azharites, Fifteen Years Later", pp. 139–53.

101 Ricklefs, *A History of Modern Indonesia*, p. 17. See also ibid., pp. 36–58.

102 See Azra, *The Transmission of Islamic Reform to Indonesia*, p. 18; Drewes "New Light on the Coming of Islam to Indonesia ?", 2001, pp. 133–4.

103 Johns, "Islam in Southeast Asia", p. 406.

104 Christine Dobbin, *Islamic Revivalism in a Changing Peasant Economy: Central Sumatra, 1784–1847*, Scandinavian Institute of Asian Studies, Monograph Series no. 47 (London and Malmo: Curzon Press, 1983), pp. 117–224; Christine Dobbin, "Islamic Revivalism in Minangkabau at the Turn of the Nineteenth Century", *Modern Asian Studies*, vol. 8, no. 3 (1974), pp. 319–56; Taufik Abdullah, "Adat and Islam: An Examination of Conflict in Minangkabau", *Indonesia*, II (October 1966), pp. 1–24; Taufik Abdullah, "Modernization in the Minangkabau World: West Sumatra in the Early Decades of the Twentieth Century", in *Culture and Politics in Indonesia*, edited by Claire Holt (Ithaca: Cornell University Press, 1972), pp. 198–205; Roff, "South-East Asian Islam in the Nineteenth Century", pp. 155–70; Johns, "Islam in Southeast Asia", p. 410; Azra, *The Transmission of Islamic Reform to Indonesia*, pp. 549–66; Benda, "South-East Asian Islam in the Twentieth Century", p. 182.

105 See Kartodirdjo, *The Peasant's Revolt of Banten in 1888*, pp. 140–75.

106 Clive J. Christie, *A Modern History of Southeast Asia: Decolonization, Nationalism and Separatism* (London; New York; I.B. Tauris Publishers, 1996), pp. 141–3, 146, 248 note 20; Carl A. Trocki, "Political Structures in the Nineteenth and Early Twentieth Centuries", in *The Cambridge History of Southeast Asia*, vol. Two: *The Nineteenth and Twentieth Centuries*, edited by Nicholas Tarling (Cambridge: Cambridge University Press, 1992), pp. 104–5; Roff,

"South-East Asian Islam in the Nineteenth Century", pp. 179–80; van Dijk, "Colonial Fears, 1890–1918", pp. 59–60. See also Watson and Ishii, "Religious Developments in Southeast Asia", p. 520; Bernard Lewis, *What Went Wrong? Western Impact and Middle Eastern Response* (London: Phoenix, 2002), pp. 15–16.

107 C. van Dijk, *Rebellion under the Banner of Islam: The Darul Islam Indonesia* (The Hague: Martinus Nijhoff, 1981), pp. 1–126. See also S. Soebardi, "Kartosuwiryo and the Darul Islam Rebellion in Indonesia", *Journal of Southeast Asian Studies*, vol. XIV, no. 1 (March 1983), pp. 109–33; B. J. Boland, *The Struggle of Islam in Modern Indonesia* (The Hague: Martinus Nijhoff, 1971), pp. 54–75; van Bruinessen, "Genealogies", p.119.

108 See van Dijk, *Rebellion under the Banner of Islam*, pp. 127–339.

109 See ICG, *Al-Qaeda in Southeast Asia*; van Bruinessen, "Genealogies", pp. 128–30, 146.

110 Lawrence, *Defenders of God*, p. 100.

111 See ibid., pp. 90–101.

112 See Marty and Appleby, "Conclusions", p. 816.

113 Ibid., p. 814.

114 Carré, *Mysticism and Politics*, pp. 2–3, 8.

115 van Dijk, *Rebellion under the Banner of Islam*, pp. 23–34; Noer, *The Modernist Muslim Movement in Indonesia*, p. 134, note. 137. See also Effendy, *Islam and the State in Indonesia*, p. 19.

116 van Dijk, *Rebellion under the Banner of Islam*, p. 34.

117 Ibid. See also Noer, *The Modernist Muslim Movement in Indonesia*, pp. 144–8.

118 Peter G. Riddell, *Islam and the Malay-Indonesian World*, p. 8.

Chapter III   Radical Islamic Fundamentalism: The Distinctiveness of the Indonesian Context

Epigraph: Robert W. Hefner, "Modernity and the Challenge of Pluralism: Some Indonesian Lessons", *Studia Islamika*, vol. 2, no. 4 (1995), p. 41.

1   See ICG (International Crisis Group), *Indonesia: Violence and Radical Muslims*, ICG Indonesia Briefing (Jakarta/Brussels, ICG, October 10, 2001), pp, 2, 16 (this paper can be found at the ICG website at: *http://www.crisisweb.org/projects/reports.cfm*); ICG (International Crisis Group), *Al-Qaeda in Southeast Asia: The Case of the "Ngruki Network" in Indonesia,* ICG Indonesia Briefing (Jakarta/Brussels: ICG, August 8, 2002), p. 1 (this paper can be found at the ICG website at: *http://www.crisisweb.org/projects/reports.cfm*); Greg Barton, "The Prospects for Islam", in *Indonesia Today: Challenges of History*, edited

by Garson Lloyd and Shannon Smith (Singapore: Institute Southeast Asian Studies, 2001), pp. 248–9; Greg Barton, "Islamism and Indonesia: Islam and the Contest for Power after Suharto", July 9, 2003 (see on-line at: *http://www.gusdur.net/english/ english_detail.asp? contentOID=50*); Greg Barton, "Assessing the Threat of Radical Islamism in Indonesia", pp. 1–2 (see on-line at: *http://www.sisr.net/apo/ Islamism_in_Indonesia.rtf*); Harold Crouch, "Qaida in Indonesia? The Evidence Doesn't Support Worries", *International Herald Tribune*, October 23, 2001; Rohan Gunaratna, *Inside Al Qaeda: Global Network of Terror* (New York: Columbia University Press, 2002), p. 198.

2 See Michael Davis, "Laskar Jihad and the Political Position of Conservative Islam in Indonesia", *Contemporary Southeast Asia*, vol. 24, no. 1 (April 2002).

3 Greg Fealy, "Islamic Politics: A Rising or Declining Force ?", in *Indonesia: The Uncertain Transition*, edited by Damien Kingsbury and Arief Budiman (Adelaide: Crawford House Publishing, 2001), p. 119.

4 Ibid., "Islamic Politics", p. 126. See also Greg Barton, "Islam, Politics, and Regime Change in Wahid's Indonesia", in *Tiger's Roar: Asia's Recovery and its Impact*, edited by Julian Weiss (Armonk: M.E. Sharpe, 2001), p. 314.

5 Andreas Harsono, "Islamic Parties May Be Big Losers in Indonesian Elections", *The American Reporter*, vol. 10, no. 2,351, April 26, 2004 (see on-line at: *http://www.american-reporter.com/2,351/39.html*); Rob Taylor, "Islam not Selling in Indonesian Elections", *AAP Newsfeed*, March 26, 2004; Mafoot Simon, "Parties Drop Religious Issues", *The Straits Times*, April 2, 2004.

6 See Hyung-Jun Kim, "The Changing Interpretation of Religious Freedom in Indonesia", *Journal of Southeast Asian Studies*, vol. 29, no. 2 (September 1998), pp. 357–73.

7 See Emmanuel Sivan, *Radical Islam: Medieval Theology and Modern Politics*, enlarged edition (New Haven and London: Yale University Press, 1990), pp. 40–7; Sana Abed-Kotob, "The Accommodationists Speak: Goals and Strategies of the Muslim Brotherhood of Egypt", *International journal of Middle East Studies*, vol. 27 (1995), p. 332.

8 See Robert W. Hefner, *Civil Islam: Muslims and Democratization in Indonesia* (Princeton and Oxford: Princeton University Press, 2000), pp. 128–66; Greg Barton, "Islamic Liberalism and the Prospects for Democracy in Indonesia", pp. 440–1; Bahtiar Effendy, *Islam and the State in Indonesia* (Singapore: Institute of Southeast Asian Studies, 2003), pp. 172–7.

9 See Olivier Roy, *The Failure of Political Islam* (Cambridge, MA: Harvard University Press, 1994), pp. 44–7.

10 See Saad Eddin Ibrahim, "Egypt's Islamic Activism in the 1980s", *Third World Quarterly*, vol. 10, no. 2 (April 1988), p. 646.

11 Mathias Diederich, "A Closer Look at *Dakwah* and Politics in Indonesia: The *Partai Keadilan*", *Archipel*, 64 (2002), p. 111.

12 Noorhaidi Hasan, "Faith and Politics: The Rise of The Laskar Jihad in The Era of Transition in Indonesia, *Indonesia*, 73 (April 2002), p. 162.

13 Krishna Sen, "Gendered Citizens in the New Indonesian Democracy", *Rima*, vol. 36, no. 1 (2002), p. 55.

14 Martin van Bruinessen, "Genealogies of Islamic Radicalism in post-Suharto Indonesia", *South East Asia Research*, vol. 10, no. 2 (July 2002), p. 145.

15 See Roy, *The Failure of Political Islam*, p. 14.

16 See R. William Liddle, *Leadership and Culture in Indonesian Politics* (Sydney: Asian Studies Association of Australia in association with Allen & Unwin, 1996), p. 77; Barton, "Islam, Politics, and Regime Change in Wahid's Indonesia", p. 313.

17 ICG (International Crisis Group), *Indonesia: The Search for Peace in Maluku*, ICG Asia Report, no. 31 (Jakarta/Brussels: ICG, 8 February, 2002 – this paper can be found at the ICG website at: *http://www. crisisweb.org/projects/reports.cfm*); ICG (International Crisis Group) *Indonesia: Overcoming Murder and Chaos in Maluku*, ICG Asia Report, no. 10 (Jakarta/Brusseles: ICG, 19 December, 2000 – this paper can be found at the ICG website at: *http://www.crisisweb. org/projects/reports.cfm*); Chris Wilson, *International Conflicts in Indonesia: Causes, Symptoms and Sustainable Resolution* (Parliament of Australia, Department of the Parliamentary Library, Research Paper 1, 2002–2), pp. 2, 10–12 (this paper can be found at the Parliament of Australia: Department of the Parliamentry Library website at: *http://www.aph.gov.au/library/pubs/rp/rp01–02.htm*); Barton, "Islam, Politics, and Regime Change in Wahid's Indonesia", p. 316; Barton, "The Prospects for Islam", p. 247.

18 See Chris Wilson, *International Conflicts in Indonesia*, pp. 4–7; B. J. Boland, *The Struggle of Islam in Modern Indonesia* (The Hague: Martinus Nijhoff, 1971), pp. 68–75; Greg Barton, " Islam and Politics in the New Indonesia", in *Islam in Asia*, edited by Jason F. Isaacson and Colin Rubenstein (New Brunswick: Transaction Publishers, 2002), pp. 52–4; Barton, "Islam, Politics, and Regime Change in Wahid's Indonesia", p. 315; ICG Asia (International Crisis Group), *Aceh: A Slim Chance for Peace*, ICG Briefing Paper (Jakarta/Brussels: ICG, 27 March, 2002), pp. 13–14 (this paper can be found at the ICG

website at: *http://www.crisisweb.org/projects/reports.cfm*); ICG, *Indonesia: Violence and Radical Muslims*, pp. 9–10; Barton, "Islam, Politics, and Regime Change in Wahid's Indonesia", pp. 31–6; Barton, "The Prospects for Islam", p. 247.

19 Robert W. Hefner, "Islam and Nation in the Post-Suharto Era", in *The Politics of Post-Suharto Indonesia*, edited by Adam Schwarz and Jonathan Paris (Singapore: Raffles, 1999), pp. 40–5; Robert W. Hefner, *Civil Islam*, p. 17.

20 Mitsuo Nakamura, "Prospects for Islam in post-Soeharto Indonesia", *Asia-Pacific Review*, vol. 6, no. 1 (1999), p. 93.

21 See Taufik Abdullah, "The Sociocultural Scene in Indonesia", in *Trends in Indonesia: Proceeding and Background Paper*, edited by Leo Suryadinata and Sharon Siddique (Singapore: Singapore University Press, 1981), p. 74; Robert W. Hefner, *Civil Islam*, p. 17.

22 See Schwarz, *A Nation in Waiting*, p. 327; Barton, "The Prospects for Islam", p. 245; Fealy, "Islamic Politics: A Rising or Declining Force?", p. 120.

23 See Roy, *The Failure of Political Islam*, pp. 31–6.

24 ICG, *Indonesia: Violence and Radical Muslims*, p. 11; ICG, *Al-Qaeda in Southeast Asia*, pp. 3–4.

25 Barton, "Islam and Politics in the New Indonesia", pp. 49–50; Barton, "Islam, Politics, and Regime Change in Wahid's Indonesia", p. 314. See also Dini Djalal, "The Past Catches Up", *Far Eastern Economic Review*, issue 45, vol. 165 (November 14, 2002), pp. 18–19.

26 See Effendy, *Islam and the State in Indonesia*, pp. 13–64.

27 See Hefner, *Civil Islam*, pp. 16–20, 94–171.

28 See Bahtiar Effendy, "Islam and the State in Indonesia: Munawir Sjadzali and the Development of a New Theological Underpinning of Political Islam", *Studia Islamika*, vol. 2, no. 2, (1995), pp. 101–2; Bahtiar Effendy, *Islam and the State in Indonesia*, pp. 13–64; M. Din Syamsuddin, "Islamic Political Thought and Cultural Revival in Modern Indonesia"; Kim, "The Changing Interpretation of Religious Freedom in Indonesia"; ICG, *Indonesia: Violence and Radical Muslims*, p. 15; B. J. Boland, *The Struggle of Islam in Modern Indonesia*, pp. 165–74.

29 See Effendy, *Islam and the State in Indonesia*, pp. 65–123; Effendy, "Islam and the State in Indonesia", pp. 97–121; M. Din Syamsuddin, "Islamic Political Thought and Cultural Revival in Modern Indonesia", *Studia Islamika*, vol. 2, no. 4 (1995), pp. 47–68; Greg Barton, "Neo-Modernism: A Vital Synthesis of Traditionalist and Modernist Islamic Thought in Indonesia", *Studia Islamika*, vol. 2, no.

3 (1995), pp. 1–75; Barton, "Islamic Liberalism and the Prospects for Democracy in Indonesia", p. 435.

30 See Effendy, *Islam and the State in Indonesia*, pp. 102–23; Effendy, "Islam and the State in Indonesia", pp. 97–121; Syamsuddin, "Islamic Political Thought and Cultural Revival in Modern Indonesia", pp. 47–68; Barton, "Neo-Modernism", pp. 1–75; Hendro Prasetyo, "Interview with Munawir Sjadazli", *Studia Islamika*, vol. 1, no. 1 (April–June 1994), pp. 185–205. About the Medina Charter, see Ali Bulac, "The Medina Document", in *Liberal Islam: A Sourcebook*, edited by Charles Kurzman (New York: Oxford University Press, 1988), pp. 169–78.

31 For the terms "desacralization, "reactualization" and "indigeniza-tion", see Effendy, *Islam and the State in Indonesia*, pp. 65–80. For the term "reactualization" see also R. Michael Feener, *Developments of Muslim Jurisprudence in Twentieth Century Indonesia* (Ph.D. dissertation, Boston: Boston University, 1999), 142–95, 243–4.

32 See Barton, "Neo-Modernism", pp.1–75; Barton, "Islamic Liberalism and the Prospects for Democracy in Indonesia", pp. 427–51.

33 See Charles Kurzman, "Introduction: Liberal Islam and its Islamic Context", in *Liberal Islam: A Sourcebook*, edited by Charles Kurzman (New York: Oxford University Press, 1988), pp. 3–26; Nurcholish Madjid, "The Necessity of Renewing Islamic Thought and Reinvigorating Religious Understanding", in *Liberal Islam: A Sourcebook*, edited by Charles Kurzman, pp. 284–94; Greg Barton, "Islam and Politics in the New Indonesia", pp. 16–21; Barton, "Islamic Liberalism and the Prospects for Democracy in Indonesia", 427–51.

34 See Bahtiar Effendy, *Islam and the State: The Transformation of Islamic Political Ideas and Practices in Indonesia* (Ph.D. dissertation, The Ohio State University, 1994, pp. 47–50); Fealy, "Islamic Politics: A Rising or Declining Force ?", p. 120.

35 See Greg Barton, "Neo-Modernism", pp. 42–5.

36 Barton, "Islamic Liberalism and the Prospects for Democracy in Indonesia", p. 439.

37 See Azyumardi Azra, "Islam in Indonesian Foreign Policy: Assessing Impacts of Islamic Revivalism during the Soeharto Era", *Studia Islamika*, vol. 7, no. 3 (2000), p. 5.

38 Fealy, "Islamic Politics: A Rising or Declining Force ?", pp. 124–5.

39 Harsono, "Islamic Parties May Be Big Losers in Indonesian Elections".

40 See Barton, " Islam and Politics in the New Indonesia", p, 17.

41 See Martin E. Marty and R. Scott Appleby, "Conclusions: An Interim

Report on a Hypothetical Family", in *Fundamentalism Observed,* edited by Martin E. Marty and R. Scott Appleby (Chicago and London: The University of Chicago Press, 1991), p. 827.

42 Hefner, *Civil Islam*; Hefner, "Islam and Nation in the Post-Suharto Era", pp. 49, 64. See also Schwarz, *A Nation in Waiting*, pp. 328–9.

43 See Emanuel Sivan, "The Islamic Resurgence: Civil Society Strikes Back", *Journal of Contemporary History*, vol. 25 (1990), pp. 353–64.

44 See Barton, "Neo-Modernism", pp. 7–9; Barton, "Indonesia's Nurcholish Madjid and Abdurrahman Wahid as Intellectual 'Ulama': The Meeting of Islamic Traditionalism and Modernism in Neo-Modernist Thought", *Studia Islamika*, vol. 4, no. 1 (1997), p. 67; Barton, "Islamic Liberalism and the Prospects for Democracy in Indonesia", pp. 434–40.

45 See Mark W. Woodward, "Conversations with Abdurrahman Wahid", in *Toward a New Paradigm: Recent Developments in Indonesian Islamic Thought*, edited by Mark R. Woodward (Tempe: Arizona State University, Program for Southeast Asian Studies, 1996), pp. 133–53; Barton, "The Prospects for Islam", p. 252; ICG, *Indonesia: Violence and Radical Muslims*, p. 11; Christian Kiem, "Re-Islamization among Muslims Youth in Ternate Town, Eastern Indonesia", *Sojourn*, vol. 8, no. 1 (1993), p. 104.

46 See Barton, "Islam and Politics in the New Indonesia", pp. 4–5, 47–9; Marcus Mietzner, "Nationalism and Islamic Politics: Political Islam in the post-Suharto Era", in *Reformasi: Crisis and Change in Indonesia*, edited by Arief Budiman, Barbara Hatley and Damien Kingsbury (Clayton: Monash Asia Institute, 1999), pp. 179–82; ICG, *Indonesia: Violence and Radical Muslims*, p. 11; Robin L. Bush, "Redefining 'Political Islam' in Indonesia: Nahdlatul Ulama and Khittah '26", *Studia Islamika*, vol 7, no. 2 (2000), pp. 59–86.

47 Barton, "Islam and Politics in the New Indonesia", pp. 5–6, 21–3, 68.

48 See Marty and Appleby, "Conclusions", p. 831.

49 Barton, "Islamic Liberalism and the Prospects for Democracy in Indonesia", pp. 430–1.

50 Julia Day Howell, "Sufism and the Indonesian Islamic Revival", *The Journal of Asian Studies*, vol. 60, no. 3 (August 2001), pp. 701–29.

51 Robert W. Hefner, *Civil Islam*, p. 18.

52 See Barton, "Islamic Liberalism and the Prospects for Democracy in Indonesia", p. 435; Hefner, *Civil Islam,* p. 18 (see also pp. 128–213).

53 See A. H. Johns, "Perspectives of Islamic Spirituality in Southeast Asia: Reflections and Encounters", *Islam and Christian–Muslim Relations*, vol. 12, no. 1 (2001), pp. 5–21.

54 Abdullah Saeed, "Towards Religious Tolerance through Reform in Islamic Education: The Case of the State Institute of Islamic Studies of Indonesia", *Indonesia and the Malay World*, vol. 27, no. 79 (1999), pp. 177–91. See also Hefner, *Civil Islam*, p. 120.
55 Barton, "Islam and Politics in the New Indonesia", pp. 18–20; Barton, "The Prospects for Islam", p. 252.

Bibliography

Abaza, Mona, "The Discourse on Islamic Fundamentalism in the Middle East and Southeast Asia: A Critical Perspective". *Sojourn*, vol. 6, no. 2 (1991), pp. 203–39.

——, "Some Research Notes on Living Conditions and Perceptions Among Indonesian Students in Cairo". *Journal of Southeast Asia Studies*, vol. 22, no. 2 (1991), pp. 347–60.

——, *Changing Images of Three Generations of Azharites in Indonesia*. Singapore: Institute of Southeast Asian Studies, 1993.

——, "Indonesian Azharites, Fifteen Years Later", *Sojourn*, vol. 18, no. 1 (2003), pp. 139–53.

Abdullah, Taufik, "Adat and Islam: An Examination of Conflict in Minangkabau. *Indonesia*, II (October 1966), pp. 1–24.

——, "Modernization in the Minangkabau World: West Sumatra in the Early Decades of the Twentieth Century". In *Culture and Politics in Indonesia*, edited by Claire Holt. Ithaca: Cornell University Press, 1972, pp. 179–245.

——, "The Sociocultural Scene in Indonesia". In *Trends in Indonesia: Proceeding and Background Paper*, edited by Leo Suryadinata and Sharon Siddique. Singapore: Singapore University Press, 1981, pp. 65–85.

Abed-Kotob, Sana, "The Accommodationists Speak: Goals and Strategies of the Muslim Brotherhood of Egypt". *International Journal of Middle East Studies*, vol. 27 (1995), pp. 321–39.

Abu Bakar, Mohamad, "Islam and Nationalism in Contemporary Malay Society". In *Islam and Society in Southeast Asia*, edited by Taufik Abdullah and Sharon Siddique. Singapore: Institute of Southeast Asian Studies, 1986, pp. 155–74.

Abu Rabi', Ibrahim, "Christian-Muslim Relations in Indonesia: The Challenge of the Twenty-First Century. *Studia Islamika*, vol. 5, no. 1 (1998), pp. 1–23.

Adams, Charles C., *Islam and Modernism in Egypt: A Study of the Modern*

Reform Movement Inaugurated by Muhammad 'Abduh. New York: Russel & Russel, 1968.

Alatas, Syed Farid, "Hadhramaut and the Hadhrami Diaspora: Problems in Theoretical History". In *Hadhrami Traders, Scholars and Statesmen in the Indian Ocean, 1750s–1960s,* edited by Ulrike Freitag and William G. Clarence-Smith. Leiden: Brill, 1997, pp. 19–34.

al-Atsari, Dzulqarnain bin Muhammad, "Rahmat Islam Terhadap Orang Kafir". *Salafy*, 36 (2001), pp. 24–30.

Alfian, *Muhammadiyah: The Political Behavior of a Muslim Modernist Organization under Dutch Colonialism*. Yogyakarta: Gadjah Mada University Press, 1989.

Ali, Fachry and Bahtiar Effendy, *Merambah Jalan Baru Islam: Rekonstruksi Pemikiran Islam Indonesia Masa Orde Baru*. Bandung: Mizan, 1986.

Ali, Muhamad, "The Phenomenal Rise of the Prosperous Party", *The Jakarta Post*, April 20, 2004.

An-Nawawi, Abu Usamah Abdurrahman Ibnu Rawiyah, "Berlindung dari Fitnah Syirik Kufur & Munafik". *Salafy*, 36 (2001), pp. 42–4.

Andaya, Barbara Watson and Yoneo Ishii, "Religious Developments in Southeast Asia, *c.* 1500–1800". In *The Cambridge History of Southeast Asia*, vol. one, *From Early Times to c. 1800*, edited by Nicholas Tarling. Cambridge: Cambridge University Press, 1992, pp. 508–71.

Ansari, Hamied N., "The Islamic Militants in Egyptian Politics". *International Journal of Middle East Studies*, vol. 16 (1984), pp. 123–44.

As-Sewed, Muhammad Umar, "Musuh". *Buletin Laskar Jihad Ahlus Sunnah wal Jamaah*, 10, Tahun I (2001), p. 3.

——, "Sabar dalam Jihad". *Buletin Laskar Jihad Ahlus Sunnah wal Jamaah*, 15, Tahun I (2002), p. 3.

——, "Terorisme adalah Budaya Kafir". *Buletin Laskar Jihad Ahlus Sunnah wal Jamaah*, 23, Tahun II (August 2002), p. 3.

Azra, Azyumardi, *The Transmission of Islamic Reformism to Indonesia: Networks of Middle Eastern and Malay-Indonesian 'Ulama' in the Seventeenth and Eighteenth Centuries*. Ph.D. dissertation, Columbia University, 1992.

——, "The Transmission of *al-Manar*'s Reformism to the Malay-Indonesian World: The Cases of *al-Imam* and *al-Munir*". *Studia Islamika*, vol. 6, no. 3 (1999), pp. 75–100.

——, "Islam in Indonesian Foreign Policy: Assessing Impacts of Islamic Revivalism during the Soeharto Era". *Studia Islamika*, vol. 7, no. 3 (2000), pp. 3–29.

Baker, Raymond William, *Sadat and After: Struggles for Egypt's Political Soul*. Cambridge, MA: Harvard University Press, 1990.

Baried, Baroroh "Islam and the Modernization of Indonesian Women". In *Islam and Society in Southeast Asia*, edited by Taufik Abdullah and Sharon Siddique. Singapore: Institute of Southeast Asia Studies, 1986, pp. 139–54.

Barton, Greg, "Neo-Modernism: A Vital Synthesis of Traditionalist and Modernist Islamic Thought in Indonesia". *Studia Islamika*, vol. 2, no. 3 (1995), pp. 1–75.

——, "Indonesia's Nurcholish Madjid and Abdurrahman Wahid as Intellectual 'Ulama': The Meeting of Islamic Traditionalism and Modernism in neo-Modernist Thought". *Studia Islamika*, vol. 4, no. 1 (1997), pp. 29–81.

——, "Islamic Liberalism and the Prospects for Democracy in Indonesia". In *Democracy in Asia*, edited by Michèle Schmiegelow. New York: St. Martin's Press, 1997, pp. 427–51.

——, "Islam, Politics, and Regime Change in Wahid's Indonesia". In *Tiger's Roar: Asia's Recovery and its Impact*, edited by Julian Weiss. Armonk: M.E. Sharpe, 2001, pp. 312–7.

——, "The Prospects for Islam". In *Indonesia Today: Challenges of History*, edited by in Grayson Lloyd and Shannon Smith. Singapore: Institute of Southeast Asian Studies, 2001, pp. 244–55.

——, "Islam and Politics in the New Indonesia". In *Islam in Asia*, edited by Jason F. Isaacson and Colin Rubenstein. New Brunswick: Transaction Publishers, 2002, pp. 1–90.

——, "Islamism and Indonesia: Islam and the Contest for Power after Suharto", July 9, 2003 (see on-line at: *http://www.gusdur.net/english/english_detail.asp?contentOID=50*)

——, "Assessing the Threat of Radical Islamism in Indonesia" (see on-line at: *http://www.sisr.net/apo/Islamism_in_Indonesia.rtf*)

Benda, Harry J., "South-East Asian Islam in the Twentieth Century". In *The Cambridge History of Islam*, vol. 2: *The Further Islamic Lands, Islamic Society and Civilization*, edited by P. M. Holt, Ann K. S. Lambton and Bernard Lewis. London: Cambridge University Press, 1970, pp. 182–207.

Behrend, Tim, "Preaching Fundamentalism: The Public Teachings of Abu Bakar Ba'asyir". *Inside Indonesia*, no. 74 (April–June 2003), pp. 9–10.

Bluhm, Jutta E., "A Preliminary Statement on the Dialogue Established between the Reform Magazine *al-Manar* and the Malayo-Indonesian World". *Indonesia Circle*, no. 32 (November 1983), pp. 35–42.

Boland, B. J., *The Struggle of Islam in Modern Indonesia*. The Hague: Martinus Nijhoff, 1971.

Bowen, John R., "Modern Intentions: Reshaping Subjectivities in an Indonesian Muslim Society". In *Islam in an Era of Nation-States: Politics and Religious Renewal in Muslim Southeast Asia*, edited by Robert W. Hefner and Patricia Horvatich. Honolulu: University of Hawai'i Press, 1997, pp. 157–81.

Bulac, Ali, "The Medina Document". In *Liberal Islam: A Sourcebook*, edited by Charles Kurzman. New York: Oxford University Press, 1988, pp. 169–78.

Bush, Robin L. "Redefining 'Political Islam' in Indonesia: Nahdlatul Ulama and Khittah '26". *Studia Islamika*, vol. 7, no. 2 (2000), pp. 59–86.

Carré, Olivier, *Mysticism and Politics: A Critical Reading of Fi Zilal al-Qur'an by Sayyid Qutb (1906–1966)*. Translated from French by Carol Artigues and revised by W. Shepard. Leiden: Brill, 2003.

Christie, Clive J., *A Modern History of Southeast Asia: Decolonization, Nationalism and Separatism*. London and New York; I.B. Tauris Publishers, 1996.

Clarence-Smith, William G., "Hadhramaut and the Hadhrami Diaspora in the Modern Colonial Era: An Introductory Survey". In *Hadhrami Traders, Scholars and Statesmen in the Indian Ocean, 1750s–1960s*, edited by Ulrike Freitag and William G. Clarence-Smith. Leiden: Brill, 1997, pp. 1–18.

Cohen, Amnon, *Political Parties in the West Bank under the Jordanian Regime, 1949–1967*. Ithaca and London: Cornell University Press, 1980.

Cook, Michael, *Commanding Right and Forbidding Wrong in Islamic Thought*. Cambridge: Cambridge University Press, 2000.

Crouch, Harold, "Qaida in Indonesia? The Evidence Doesn't Support Worries". *International Herald Tribune*, October 23, 2001.

Davis, Michael, "Laskar Jihad and the Political Position of Conservative Islam in Indonesia". *Contemporary Southeast Asia*, vol. 24, no. 1 (April 2002), pp. 12–32.

Dekmejian, R. Hrair, *Islam in Revolution: Fundamentalism in the Arab World*. New York: Syracuse University Press, 1985.

Diederich, Mathias, "A Closer Look at *Dakwah* and Politics in Indonesia: The *Partai Keadilan*". *Archipel*, 64 (2002), pp. 101–15.

Dhume, Sadanand, "Islam Radical Appeal: Nonviolent Hizbut Tahrir is Using anti-War Sentiment to Promote Islamic Superstate". *Far Eastern Economic Review*, April 3, 2003, p. 19.

Djalal, Dini, "The Past Catches Up". *Far Eastern Economic Review*, November 14, 2002, pp. 16–19.

Dobbin, Christine, "Islamic Revivalism in Minangkabau at the Turn of the Nineteenth Century". *Modern Asian Studies*, vol. 8, no. 3 (1974), pp. 319–56.

——, *Islamic Revivalism in a Changing Peasant Economy: Central Sumatra,*

1784 1847. Scandinavian Institute of Asian Studies, Monograph Series no. 47. London and Malmo: Curzon Press, 1983.

Drewes, G. W. J., "Indonesia Mysticism and Activism". In *Unity and Variety in Muslim Civilization*, edited by Gustav E. von Grunebaum. Chicago & London: The University of Chicago Press, 1963, pp. 284–310.

——, "New Light on the Coming of Islam to Indonesia?". In *The Propagation of Islam in the Indonesian-Malay Archipelago*, edited and annotated by Alijah Gordon. Kuala Lumpur: Malaysian Sociological Research Institute, 2001, pp. 125–55.

Dzulqarnain, "Rahmat Islam di Medan Tempur". *Salafy*, 36 (2001), pp. 19–21.

Effendy, Bahtiar, *Islam and the State in Indonesia*. Singapore: Institute of Southeast Asian Studies, 2003.

——, *Islam and the State: The Transformation of Islamic Political Ideas and Practices in Indonesia*. Ph.D. dissertation, The Ohio State University, 1994.

——, "Islam and the State in Indonesia: Munawir Sjadzali and the Development of a New Theological Underpinning of Political Islam". *Studia Islamika*, vol. 2, no. 2 (1995), pp. 97–121.

Eliraz, Giora, "The Social and Cultural Conception of Mustafa Sadiq al-Rafi'i. *Asian and African Studies*, vol. 13 (1979), pp. 101–29.

——, *Egyptian Intellectuals in the Face of Tradition and Change, 1919–1939* (in Hebrew). Ph.D. dissertation, Jerusalem: The Hebrew University of Jerusalem, 1980.

Fealy, Greg, " Inside Laskar Jihad: An Interview with the Leader of a New Radical and Militant Sect". *Inside Indonesia*, no. 65 (Jan.–March 2001), pp. 28–9.

——, "Islamic Politics: A Rising or Declining Force ?". In *Indonesia: The Uncertain Transition*, edited by Damien Kingsbury and Arief Budiman. Adelaide: Crawford House Publishing, 2001, pp. 119–36.

Federspiel, Howard M., "The Muhammadijah: A Study of an Orthodox Islamic Movement in Indonesia". *Indonesia*, 10 (1970), pp. 57–79.

——, *Islam and Ideology in the Emerging Indonesian State: The Persatuan Islam (PERSIS), 1923 to 1957*. Leiden: Brill, 2001.

Feener, R. Michael, *Developments of Muslim Jurisprudence in Twentieth Century Indonesia*. Ph.D. dissertation, Boston: Boston University, 1999.

Funston, N. J., "The Origins of Parti Islam Se Malaysia". *Journal of Southeast Asian Studies*, vol. VII, no. 1 (1976), pp. 58–73.

Geertz, Clifford, *The Religion of Java*. Chicago and London: The University of Chicago, 1976.

Gershoni, Israel and James P. Jankowski, *Egypt, Islam, and the Arabs: The*

Search for Egyptian Nationhood, 1900–1930. Oxford: Oxford University Press, 1986.

Gibb, H. A. R., *Modern Trends in Islam*. Chicago: The University of Chicago Press, 1947.

Gunaratna, Rohan, *Inside Al Qaeda: Global Network of Terror*. New York: Columbia University Press, 2002.

Harsono, Andreas, "Islamic Parties May Be Big Losers in Indonesian Elections", *The American Reporter*, vol. 10, no. 2, April 26, 2004 (see online at: *http://www.american-reporter.com/2,351/39.html*).

Hasan, Noorhaidi, "Faith and Politics: The Rise of The Laskar Jihad in The Era of Transition in Indonesia. *Indonesia*, 73 (April 2002), pp. 149–69.

Hefner, Robert W., *Hindu Javanese: Tengger Tradition and Islam*. Princeton: Princeton University Press, 1985.

——, "Modernity and the Challenge of Pluralism: Some Indonesian Lessons". *Studia Islamika*, vol. 2, no. 4 (1995), pp. 21–45.

——, "Print Islam: Mass Media and Ideological Rivalries among Indonesian Muslims". *Indonesia*, 64 (October 1997), pp. 77–103.

——, "Islam in an Era of Nation-States: Politics and Religious Renewal in Muslim Southeast Asia". In *Islam in an Era of Nation-States: Politics and Religious Renewal in Muslim Southeast Asia*, edited by Robert W. Hefner and Patricia Horvatich. Honolulu: University of Hawai'i Press, 1997, pp. 3–40.

——, "Islam and Nation in the Post-Suharto Era". In *The Politics of Post-Suharto Indonesia*, edited by Adam Schwarz and Jonathan Paris. Singapore: Raffles, 1999, pp. 40–72.

——, *Civil Islam: Muslims and Democratization in Indonesia*. Princeton and Oxford: Princeton University Press, 2000.

——, "Civic Pluralism Denied? The New Media and *Jihadi* Violence in Indonesia". In *New Media in the Muslim World*, 2nd edition, edited by Dale F. Eickelman. Indiana University Press, 2003.

Hodgson, Marshall G. S., *The Venture of Islam: Conscience and History in a World Civilization*, vol. one: *The Classical Age of Islam* and vol. three: *The Gunpowder Empires and Modern Times*. Chicago: The University of Chicago Press, 1974.

Hooker, M. B., *Indonesian Islam: Social Change through Contemporary fatawa*. Crows Nest and Honolulu: Allen & Unwin and University of Hawai'i Press, 2001.

Hourani, Albert, *Arabic Thought in the Liberal Age: 1798–1939*. London: Oxford University Press, 1970.

Howell, Julia Day, "Sufism and the Indonesian Islamic Revival". *The Journal of Asian Studies*, vol. 60, no. 3 (August 2001), pp. 701–29.

Bibliography

Hurgronje, C. Snouck, *Mekka in the Latter Part of the 19th Century: Daily Life, Customs and Learning the Moslims of the East-Indian-Archipelago*. Translated by J. H. Monahan. Leiden: E.J. Brill, 1970.

Husaini, Adian, "Makna Jihad", *Buletin Laskar Jihad Ahlus Sunnah wal Jamaah*, 13, Tahun I (2001), pp. 4–5.

Ibrahim, Saad Eddin, "Islamic Militancy as a Social Movement: The Case of Two Groups in Egypt". In *Islamic Resurgence in the Arab World*, edited by Ali E. Hillal Dessouki. New York: Praeger, 1982, pp. 117–37.

———, "Egypt's Islamic Activism in the 1980s". *Third World Quarterly*, vol. 10, no. 2 (April 1988), pp. 632–57.

ICG (International Crisis Group), *Indonesia: Overcoming Murder and Chaos in Maluku*. ICG Asia Report, no. 10. Jakarta/Brussels: ICG, December 19, 2000.

———, *Indonesia: Violence and Radical Muslims*. ICG Indonesia Briefing. Jakarta/Brussels: ICG, October 10, 2001.

———, *Indonesia: The Search for Peace in Maluku*. ICG Asia Report, no. 31. Jakarta/Brussels: ICG, February 8, 2002.

———, *Aceh: A Slim Chance for Peace*. ICG Indonesia Briefing. Jakarta/Brussels: ICG, March 27, 2002.

———, *Al-Qaeda in Southeast Asia: The Case of the "Ngruki Network" in Indonesia*. ICG Indonesia Briefing. Jakarta/Brussels: ICG, August 8, 2002.

———, *Indonesia Backgrounder: How the Jemaah Islamiyah Terrorist Network Operates*. ICG Asia Report, no. 43. Jakarta/Brussels: ICG, December 11, 2002.

Ichwan, Moch Nur, "Differing Responses to an Ahmadi Translation and Exegesis: The Holy *Qur'an* in Egypt and Indonesia". *Archipel*, 62 (2001), pp. 143–61.

Johns, A. H., "Islam in Southeast Asia". In *The Encyclopedia of Religion*, edited by Mircea Eliade. New York: Macmillan Publishing Company, 1987, vol. 7, pp. 404–22.

———, "Perspectives of Islamic Spirituality in Southeast Asia: Reflections and Encounters". *Islam and Christian-Muslim Relations*, vol. 12, no. 1 (2001), pp. 5–21.

Jonge, Huub de, "Dutch Colonial Policy Pertaining to Hadhrami Immigrants". In *Hadhrami Traders, Scholars and Statesmen in the Indian Ocean, 1750s–1960s*, edited by Ulrike Freitag and William G. Clarence-Smith. Leiden: Brill, 1997, pp. 94–111.

—— and Nico Kaptein Engseng, "The Arab Presence in Southeast Asia: Some Introductory Remarks". In *Transcending Borders: Arabs, Politics, Trade and Islam in Southeast Asia*, edited by Huub De Jonge and Nico Kaptein. Leiden: KITLV Press, 2002, pp. 2–10.

Kaptein, Nico, "Meccan *Fatwas* from the End of the Nineteenth Century on Indonesia Affairs". *Studia Islamika*, vol. 2, no. 4 (1995), pp. 141–60.

Kartodirdjo, Sartono, *The Peasant's Revolt of Banten in 1888: Its Conditions, Course and Sequel: A Case Study of Social Movements in Indonesia.* 's-Gravenhage: Martinus Nijhoff, 1966.

Kepel, Gilles, *Muslim Extremism in Egypt: The Prophet and Pharaoh.* Berkeley: University of California Press, 1993.

Kern, R. A., "The Propagation of Islam in the Indonesian-Malay Archipelago". In *The Propagation of Islam in the Indonesian-Malay Archipelago.* Translated by H. M. Froger and edited and annotated by Alijah Gordon. Kuala Lumpur: Malaysian Sociological Research Institute, 2001, pp. 24–124.

Kerr, Malcolm H., *Islamic Reform: The Political and Legal Theories of Muhammad 'Abduh and Rashid Rida.* Berkeley and Los Angeles: University of California Press, 1966.

Khadduri, Majid, *War and Peace in the Law of Islam.* Baltimore: The Johns Hopkins Press, 1955.

Kiem, Christian, "Re-Islamization among Muslims Youth in Ternate Town, Eastern Indonesia". *Sojourn*, vol. 8, no. 1 (1993), pp. 92–127.

Kim, Hyung-Jun, "The Changing Interpretation of Religious Freedom in Indonesia". *Journal of Southeast Asian Studies*, vol. 29, no. 2 (1998), pp. 357–73.

Kostiner, Joseph, "Impact of the Hadrami Emigrants in the East Indies on Islamic Modernism and Social Change in the Hadramawt during the 20th Century". In *Islam in Asia*, vol. II: *Southeast and East Asia*, edited by Raphael Israeli and Anthony H. Johns. Jerusalem: The Magnes Press, 1984, pp. 206–37.

Kurzman, Charles, "Introduction: Liberal Islam and its Islamic Context". In *Liberal Islam: A Sourcebook*, edited by Charles Kurzman. New York: Oxford University Press, 1988, pp. 3–26.

Laffan, M. F., *Islamic Nationhood and Colonial Indonesia: The Umma Below the Winds.* London and New York: RoutledgeCurzon, 2003.

Lawrence, Bruce B., *Defenders of God: The Fundamentalist Revolt against the Modern Age.* San Francisco: Harper & Row, 1989.

Lewis Bernard, *What Went Wrong? Western Impact and Middle Eastern Response.* London: Phoenix, 2002.

Liddle, R. William, "*Media Dakwah* Scripturalism: One Form of Islamic Political Thought and Action in New Order Indonesia. In *Toward a New Paradigm: Recent Developments in Indonesian Islamic Thought*, edited by Mark R. Woodward. Tempe: Arizona State University, Program for Southeast Asian Studies, 1996. pp. 323–56.

——, *Leadership and Culture in Indonesian Politics*. Sydney: Asian Studies Association of Australia in association with Allen & Unwin, 1996.

Madjid, Nurcholish, "The Necessity of Renewing Islamic Thought and Reinvigorating Religious Understanding". In *Liberal Islam: A Sourcebook*, edited by Charles Kurzman. New York: Oxford University Press, 1988, pp. 284–94.

Mandal, Sumit K., "Natural Leaders of Native Muslims: Arab Ethnicity and Politics in Java under Dutch Rule". In *Hadhrami Traders, Scholars and Statesmen in the Indian Ocean, 1750s–1960s*, edited by Ulrike Freitag and William G. Clarence-Smith. Leiden: Brill, 1997, pp. 185–98.

——, "Forging a Modern Arab Identity in Java in the Early Twentieth Century". In *Transcending Borders: Arabs, Politics, Trade and Islam in Southeast Asia*, edited by Huub De Jonge and Nico Kaptein. Leiden: KITLV Press, 2002, pp. 163–84.

Marty, Martin E., and R. Scott Appleby, "Conclusions: An Interim Report on a Hypothetical Family". In *Fundamentalism Observed,* edited by Martin E. Marty and R. Scott Appleby. Chicago and London: The University of Chicago Press, 1991, pp. 814–42.

McVey, Ruth, " Faith as the Outsider: Islam in Indonesian Politics". In *Islam in the Political Process*, edited by James P. Piscatori. Cambridge: Cambridge University Press, 1983, pp.194–225.

Mietzner, Marcus, "Nationalism and Islamic Politics: Political Islam in the post-Suharto Era". In *Reformasi: Crisis and Change in Indonesia*, edited by Arief Budiman, Barbara Hatley and Damien Kingsbury (Clayton: Monash Asia Institute, 1999), pp. 173–211.

Milner, Anthony, "Islam and the Muslim State". In *Islam in South-East Asia*, edited by M. B. Hooker. Leiden: E.J. Brill, 1983, pp. 23–49.

——, *The Invention of Politics in Colonial Malaya: Contesting Nationalism and the Expansion of the Public Sphere*. Cambridge: Cambridge University Press, 1994.

Mobini-Kesheh, Natalie, "Islamic Modernism in Colonial Java: The al-Irshad Movement". In *Hadhrami Traders, Scholars and Statesmen in the Indian Ocean, 1750s–1960s*, edited by Ulrike Freitag and William G. Clarence-Smith. Leiden: Brill, 1997, pp. 231–48.

——, *The Hadrami Awakening : Community and Identity in the Netherlands East Indies, 1900–1942*. Ithaca: Cornell University Press, 1999.

Mutalib, Hussin, *Islam in Malaysia: From Revivalism to Islamic State*. Singapore: Singapore University Press, 1993.

Nagata, Judith, "The New Fundamentalism; Islam in Contemporary Malaysia". *Asian Thought & Society*, vol. V, no. 14 (1980), pp. 128–41.

Nair, Shanti, *Islam in Malaysian Foreign Policy*. London and New York: Routledge, 1997.

Nakamura, Mitsuo, "Prospects for Islam in post-Soeharto Indonesia". *Asia-Pacific Review*, vol. 6, no. 1 (1999), pp. 89–108.

Noer, Deliar, *The Modernist Muslim Movement in Indonesia, 1900–1942.* Oxford: Oxford University Press, 1978.

——, "Contemporary Political Dimensions of Islam". In *Islam in South-East Asia*, edited by M. B. Hooker. Leiden: E.J. Brill, 1983, pp. 183–215.

Nurwahid, Hidayat & Zulkieflimansyan, "The Justice Party and Democracy: A Journey of a Thousand Miles Starts with a Single Step", in *Piety and Pragmatism: Trends in Indonesian Islamic Politics,* Special Report, edited by Amy McCreedy, Woodrow Wilson Center, Asia Program, April 2003, pp. 20–2 (see on-line at: *http://wwics.si.edu/topics/pubs/asiarpt_110.pdf*)

Paz, Reuven, "Global Jihad and the United States: Interpretation of the New World Order of Usama Bin Ladin". *PRISM Series of Global Jihad*, no. 1, February 2003 (see on-line at: *http://gloria.idc.ac.il/islam/global_jihad.html*)

Peacock, James L., *Consciousness and Change: Symbolic Anthropology in Evolutionary Perspective*. Oxford: Basil Blackwell, 1975.

——, *Muslim Puritans: Reformist Psychology in Southeast Asian Islam.* Berkeley: University of California Press, 1978.

——, *Purifying the Faith: The Muhammadijah Movement in Indonesian Islam.* Menlo Park: The Benjamin/Cummings Publishing House, 1978.

Prasetyo, Hendro, "Interview with Munawir Sjadazli". *Studia Islamika*, vol. 1, no. 1 (April–June 1994), pp. 185–205.

Qutb, Sayid [Sayyid], *Petunjuk Jalan.* Alih bahasa, A. Rahman Zainuddin. Jakarta: Media Dakwah, 1980.

——, *Social Justice in Islam.* Translated from the Arabic by John B. Hardie. Translation revised and introduction by Hamid Algar. Oneonta: Islamic Publications International, 2000.

Rahardgo, M. Dawam, "Perceptions of Culture in the Islamic Movement: An Indonesian Perspective". *Sojourn*, vol. 7, no. 2 (August 1992), pp. 248–73.

Rais, M. Amien, "International Islamic Movements and Their Influence upon Islamic Movement in Indonesia". *Prisma*, no. 35 (March 1985), pp. 27–48.

Ramage, Duglas E. *Politics in Indonesia: Democracy, Islam and the Ideology of Tolerance*, London: Routledge, 1997.

Reid, Anthony, "Introduction". In *The Making of an Islamic Political Discourse in Southeast Asia*, edited by Anthony Reid. Monash Papers on Southeast Asia – no. 27. Clayton: Monash University, 1993, pp. 1–15.

Ricklefs, M. C., A History of Modern Indonesia: Since *c.* 1200, 3rd edition. Stanford: Stanford University Press, 2001.

, "Six Centuries of Islamization in Java". In *Conversion to Islam*, edited by Nehemia Levtzion. New York: Holmes & Meier Publishers, 1979, pp. 100–28.

Riddell, Peter G., "Religious Links between Hadhramaut and the Malay-Indonesian World, *c.* 1850 to *c.* 1950". In *Hadhrami Traders, Scholars and Statesmen in the Indian Ocean, 1750s–1960s*, edited by Ulrike Freitag and William G. Clarence-Smith. Leiden: Brill, 1997, pp. 217–30.

——, "Arab Migrants and Islamization in the Malay World during the Colonial Period". *Indonesia and the Malay World*, vol. 29, no. 84 (2001), pp. 113–28.

——, *Islam and the Malay-Indonesian World: Transmission and Responses.* Honolulu: University of Hawai'i Press, 2001.

Roff, William R., "Kaum Muda – Kaum Tua: Innovation and Reaction Amongst the Malays, 1900–1941". In *Papers on Malayan History*, edited by K. G. Tregonning. Singapore: Journal South-East Asian History, 1962, pp. 162–92.

——, *The Origins of Malay Nationalism.* New Haven and London: Yale University Press, 1967.

——, "Indonesian and Malay Students in Cairo in the 1920's". *Indonesia*, 9 (1970), pp. 73–87.

——, "South-East Asian Islam in the Nineteenth Century". In *The Cambridge History of Islam*, vol. 2: *The Further Islamic Lands, Islamic Society and Civilization*, edited by P. M. Holt, Ann K. S. Lambton and Bernard Lewis. London: Cambridge University Press, 1970, pp. 155–81.

——, *Bibliography of Malay and Arabic Periodicals Published in the Straits Settlements and Peninsular Malay States, 1876–1941.* London: Oxford University Press, 1972.

——, "Murder as an Aid to Social History: The Arabs in Singapore in the Early Twentieth Century". In *Transcending Borders: Arabs, Politics, Trade and Islam in Southeast Asia*, edited by Huub De Jonge and Nico Kaptein. Leiden: KITLV Press: 2002, pp. 91–108.

Roy, Olivier, *The Failure of Political Islam.* Cambridge, MA: Harvard University Press, 1994.

Safran, Nadav, *Egypt in Search of Political Community: An Analysis of the Intellectual and Political Evolution of Egypt, 1904–1952.* Cambridge, MA: Harvard University Press, 1961.

Saeed, Abdullah, "Towards Religious Tolerance through Reform in Islamic Education: The Case of the State Institute of Islamic Studies of Indonesia". *Indonesia and the Malay World*, vol. 27, no. 79 (1999), pp. 177–91.

Schwarz Adam, *A Nation in Waiting: Indonesia's Search for Stability*, 2nd edition. Boulder, CO: Westview Press, 2000.

Sen, Krishna, "Gendered Citizens in the New Indonesian Democracy". *Rima*, vol. 36, no. 1 (2002), pp. 51–65.

Sholeh, Badrus, "Islamic Forces in Maluku". Unpublished paper presented at workshop on "The Dynamics of Political Islam in Indonesia", organized by Melbourne University and Melbourne Indonesia Consortium Conference, Malbourne, July 2003.

Siddiqe, Sharon, "Conceptualizing Contemporary Islam: Religion or Ideology". *Annual Review of the Social Sciences of Religion*, vol. 5. The Hague: Moulton, 1981, pp. 203–23.

Simon, Mafoot, "Parties Drop Religious Issues", *The Straits Times*, April 2, 2004.

Sivan, Emmanuel, *Radical Islam : Medieval Theology and Modern Politics*. Enlarged edition. New Haven and London: Yale University Press, 1990.

——, "The Islamic Resurgence: Civil Society Strikes Back". *Journal of Contemporary History,* vol. 25 (1990), pp. 353–64.

Soebardi, S., "Kartosuwiryo and the Darul Islam Rebellion in Indonesia". *Journal of Southeast Asian Studies*, vol. XIV, no. 1 (March 1983), pp. 109–33.

Stockwell, A. J., "Imperial Security and Moslem Militancy, With Special Reference to the Hertogh Riots in Singapore (December 1950)". *Journal of Southeast Asian Studies*, vol. XVII, no. 2 (1986), pp. 322–35.

Syamsuddin, M. Din, *Religion and Politics in Islam: The Case of Muhammadiyah in Indonesia*'s *New Order*. Ph.D. dissertation, Los Angeles: University of California, 1991.

——, "The Muhammadiyah Da'wah and Allocative Politics in the New Order Indonesia". *Studia Islamika*, vol. 2, no. 2 (1995), pp. 35–71.

——, "Islamic Political Thought and Cultural Revival in Modern Indonesia". *Studia Islamika*, vol. 2, no. 4 (1995), pp. 47–68.

Taylor Rob, "Islam not Selling in Indonesian Elections", *AAP Newsfeed*, March 26, 2004.

Text of "Declaration of War" by the Leader of Laskar Jihad. BBC Monitoring International Reports, 16 May, 2002 (see on-line at: *http://www.infid.be/wardeclaration.html*).

Thalib, Ja'far Umar, "Makar". *Buletin Laskar Jihad Ahlus Sunnah wal Jamaah*, 5, Tahun I (2001), p. 6.

——, "Merapikan Barisan Muslimin Menghadapi Permusuhan Salibis dan Zionis International". *Buletin Laskar Jihad Ahlus Sunnah wal Jamaah*, 25, Tahun II (4–17 Oktober 2002), pp. 4–5.

——, "Munafiq". *Buletin Laskar Jihad Ahlus Sunnah wal Jamaah*, 6, Tahun I (2001), p. 7.

Transcript of Abu Bakar's Comment, December 13, 2002 (see on-line at: *http://smh.com.au/articles/2002/12/13/1039656177555.html*).

Trocki, Carl A., "Political Structures in the Nineteenth and Early Twentieth Centuries". In *The Cambridge History of Southeast Asia*, vol. Two: *The Nineteenth and Twentieth Centuries*, edited by Nicholas Tarling. Cambridge: Cambridge University Press, 1992, pp. 79–130.

Tyan, E., "Djihad". In *The Encyclopaedia of Islam*, edited by B. Lewis, Ch. Pellat and J. Schacht. New edition. Leiden: E.J. Brill and London: Luzac & Co., 1965, pp. 538–40.

van Bruinessen, Martin, "Muslims of the Dutch East Indies and the Caliphate Question. *Studia Islamika*, vol. 2, no. 3 (1995), pp. 115–40.

——, "Genealogies of Islamic Radicalism in post-Suharto Indonesia". *South East Asia Research*, vol. 10, no. 2 (July 2002), pp. 117–54.

——, "Post-Suharto Muslim Engagements with Civil Society and Democracy", paper presented at the Third International Conference and Workshop "Indonesia in Transition", organized by the KNAW and Labsosio, Universitas Indonesia, August 24–28, 2003. Universitas Indonesia, Depok (see on-line at: *http://www.let.uu.nl/~martin.vanbruinessen/personal/publications/Post_Suharto_Islam_and_civil_society.htm*).

van Dijk, C., *Rebellion under the Banner of Islam: The Darul Islam Indonesia*. The Hague: Martinus Nijhoff, 1981.

——, "Colonial Fears, 1890–1918: Pan-Islamism and the Germano-Indian Plot". In *Transcending Borders: Arabs, Politics, Trade and Islam in Southeast Asia*, edited by Huub De Jonge and Nico Kaptein. Leiden: KITLV Press: 2002, pp. 53–89.

von der Mehden, Fred R, "Islamic Resurgence in Malaysia". In *Islam and Development: Religion and Sociopolitical Change*, edited by John L. Esposito. New York: Syracuse University Press, 1980, pp. 163–80.

——, "The Political and Social Challenge of the Islamic Revival in Malaysia and Indonesia". *The Muslim World*, vol. LXXVI, nos. 3–4 (1986), pp. 219–33.

——, *Religion and Modernization in Southeast Asia*. Syracuse: Syracuse University Press, 1986.

——, *Two Worlds of Islam: Interaction between Southeast Asia and the Middle East*. Gainesville: University Press of Florida, 1993.

Voll, John O., "Fundamentalism in the Sunni Arab World: Egypt and the Sudan". In *Fundamentalism Observed,* edited by Martin E. Marty and R. Scott Appleby. Chicago and London: The University of Chicago Press, 1991, pp. 345–402.

Weyland, Petra, "International Muslim Networks and Islam in Singapore". *Sojourn*, vol. 5, no. 2 (1990), pp. 219–54.

Watson, Barbara Andaya and Yoneo Ishii, "Religious Developments in

Southeast Asia, c.1500–1800". In *The Cambridge History of Southeast Asia*, vol. one: *From Early Times to c. 1800*, edited by Nicholas Tarling. Cambridge: Cambridge University Press, 1992, pp. 508–71.

Wilson, Chris, *International Conflicts in Indonesia: Causes, Symptoms and Sustainable Resolution*. Research Paper 1 2001–2. Parliament of Australia, Department of the Parliamentary Library (see on-line at: *http://www.aph.gov.au/library/pubs/rp/2001–02/02RP01.htm*).

Woodward, Mark R., "Conversations with Abdurrahman Wahid". In *Toward a New Paradigm: Recent Developments in Indonesian Islamic Thought*, edited by Mark R. Woodward. Tempe: Arizona State University, Program for Southeast Asian Studies, 1996, pp. 133–53.

——, *Islam In Java: Normative Piety and Mysticism in the Sultanate of Yogyakarta*. Tucson: The University of Arizona Press, 1989.

Index

Index

Index